Sadly passed away
03 AUGUST 2024

CW00740642

No thank you to chemotherapy and radiation.
10+ years later and I am standing right here offering you...

Practical Hope

Mrs. Daleen M. Wilson
with Mr. Bruce J. Wilson

Practical Hope

Daleen Wilson

ISBN: 979-8-89342-465-2

© 2024. All rights reserved. No part of this publication may be reproduced, distributed, or transmitted in any form or by any means, including photocopying, recording, or other electronic or mechanical methods, without the prior written permission of the publisher, except in the case of brief quotations embodied in critical reviews and certain other noncommercial uses permitted by copyright law.

Dedication

This book is dedicated to Mr. Right. He helped save my life. Mr. Right was the one, the only one who believed in my choice. He gave me wings to fly and a safety net in case I stumbled. I love that man with my whole being.

These words are dedicated to Zoe, Adelaide, Cooper and Hunter. You were the first people I thought of the moment after I was given my diagnosis. You are each MAGNIFICENT souls with unlimited healing potential. You make my life Grand!

The following chapters are dedicated to you. Yes, you there, you brave soul holding this book. Someone who is quietly interested in seeking health, wellness and vitality, a person who is curious and open minded and not afraid of change. A person who has a feeling there are hundreds of natural healing methods along the path less traveled and is seeking Practical Hope.

Index

Introduction

More than likely, you picked up this book because you, your loved one or friend, have been given a less than positive health diagnosis. (Or, if you picked it up to support and encourage me, thank you. I appreciate your kindness.)

Before we begin, I am sincerely sorry you have been given a scary scenario. That moment and those harsh words will bring even the toughest among us to our knees.

I am quite sure your heart is racing, and your brain is swirling or maybe completely foggy. It is NOT a contest as to what the diagnosis is. Weather you heard the words; unique, rare, diabetes, dementia, heart issues, hearing issues, stroke, dental problems, kidney issues, or cancer. To each person, the words are scary and most likely out of your wheelhouse.

You might feel like you are griping and hanging on to a thick, long, twisted, scratchy rope, you are swinging over a deep, dark pool of water.......... and at some point, you are going to have to let go.

> "Whatever you do, you need courage. Whatever course you decide upon, there is always someone to tell you that you are wrong. There are always difficulties arising that tempt you to believe your critics are right."
>
> RALPH WALDO EMERSON

As you already know, I chose the path that was less travelled. I do not believe that you can poison yourself back to health. You might have already guessed there are countless people who have told me I am wrong.

I felt a tap on my shoulder; I pretended not to hear my calling. After dragging my feet, coming up with many excuses, I embarked upon writing a book. Currently, you have that book in your red, hot, swollen (from clutching that rope) hands.

This book – any book is a starting point. I ask you to challenge what you read. **Please do not take my word for it.** In the process of your researching further, you will become educated on the subject. It is worth taking the time and putting forth due diligence to learn about healing. You can then make wise, informed health choices for yourself.

I was thinking back when I let go of my rope. I wished there was a beginner guide-book I could flip through and get a few answers. Maybe nothing too heavy, as my heart and soul were already hurt and bruised from my cancer diagnosis. I craved someone who had "been there, done that". To begin, I needed some small, quick, easy, common sense, faith backed, solutions, positive thoughts, remedies and a list of suggestions. I needed and wanted some ideas gathered together in one book, a place to begin. Maybe something I could actually do today?

There will be plenty of time ahead to dig deep into the serious, heavy material. However, to begin with, having some Practical Hope sounds like a good place to start.

I was panicked, nervous, scared and bamboozled. What am I going to do? Where do I begin? Can I heal myself? (Spoiler alert...good news ending...YES, **you can heal yourself!**)

I was in search of answers. Originally, I thought I needed them fast. 10 plus years later, I calmed down and realized that I needed ideas and helpful suggestions, not necessarily fast.

I will share my list of 80+ books and the authors' names that have inspired and educated me in some fashion.

Some authors literally helped save my life. (Side note: Yes, I have sent heartfelt and sincere thank you notes.) Others shared one simple idea, technique or action that switched my thinking and direction toward better health. Quite a few of the books I list offer solutions and remedies and were of tremendous help. And, yes, there are a couple books that were not my cup of tea.

I will share "The List" of 200+ things I changed for a more positive, healthy, vibrant life.

I will share some of the protocols that I tried; and some I continue to use today, to heal my body.

Of course, I will tuck in some personal stories that may encourage you and offer ideas and solutions, maybe even make you laugh. Oh yes, let me be the first to let you in on a secret….laughter will help heal your body, mind and soul.

At the end of most chapters, I will offer, what I like to refer to as: **Gentle Suggestions.** You won't find any finger pointing here. We are walking down this road together. No judgment. Isn't that refreshing? Just hand holding while offering Practical Hope and helpful ideas. Heck, that alone is worth reading the book.

It is not my place to tell you what to do. At times I cringe and wish I could shake people and tell them they are headed in the wrong direction. However, I hold my tongue. I certainly do not relish the idea of people telling me what to do and what I did wrong. Consequently, I do not want to tell anyone what they should do.

"Nobody cures you; you cure yourself"

DR. MINDY PELZ

I promise to stand in your corner, quietly encouraging you. I will offer up as much support and hope that these pages will hold. Even when every other human slowly slips away, I promise to be there, through these pages, lifting up your spirit. You can count on me.

A little bit of courage, begets courage. **Show courage where God has you right now**. God will Bless that. You may not know or understand where this is all going. But stand in that courage.

Please don't get stuck because of fear.

Gentle Suggestion (and here we go...)

"Your illness does not define you. Your
strength and courage do."

LEE SERPA AZEVADO

Foreword

Before you begin, do yourself a favor, if you have been given a diagnosis of any kind and you picked up this book in need of a smidgen of hope, give yourself a little grace and skip the chapter, "My Story". I am serious.

I promise, in 3 years when you are feeling healthier, more stable on your feet, less teary eyed and more curious about my story the chapter will still be here. The book may have fallen behind the bookcase, covered in cobwebs, but it will be there. You DO NOT need to read my sad-faced story right now; it will only bring you down.

From this moment on, the rest of the pages are filled with **Practical Hope**.

Not just pie in the sky hope. Not the words on a fancy store-bought card that read "I hope you feel better." Actual things that I did, that maybe you could try, and they too will bring your ideas for your own healing and wellness.

My initial diagnosis was Hypothyroidism and Breast Cancer. The doctors told Mr. Right "If she doesn't have surgery, chemotherapy and radiation, she won't live to see Christmas."

I said no, thank you.

As I write this, it is 10+ years later and surprise, surprise...

I am STANDING RIGHT HERE!

I am OFFERING YOU HOPE!

You DID NOT receive a death sentence.

NO ONE, I REPEAT NO ONE knows our expiration date. No human has the right or knowledge to tell you the month you will expire.

I firmly believe with my entire being that only God has numbered our days.

Dr. Bradford Weeks said something that gave me reason to pause and re-evaluate.

Someone in a white coat with that authority who says, "You have 6 weeks to live" THAT is assault with a deadly weapon. That must stop.

Okay, back to living a normal life.

Unfortunately, you will still need to pay your taxes. You <u>will</u> (I underlined that for you, you're welcome) have the opportunity to figure out how to achieve your goal of golfing in all 50 states. How to fill your goal of owning a seafood bistro, recording a song, writing a book, watching a national league hockey game in every team's home arena, or opening your own yoga studio.

Yes, the search & work continues...I continue trying to make the elusive perfect pizza crust.

On the following pages, I would like to share practical ideas, gentle suggestions, books, tips, websites and names of people who helped me get back to living a hopeful, vibrant, gracious, grateful life.

Oh, wait! You weren't living a Gracious, Grateful, Thriving, Vibrant, HOPE-filled life before your diagnosis?... note to self: five things I need to change, starting now!

I am not going to spoon feed you what to do and how to do it. Rather I thought I would share several gentle suggestions of resources to help you as you increase your health. Gather and read from as many sources as possible. Trust no one. Do your own due diligence. Trust but verify.

Today, forward...............We Live in Hope.

"Just as despair can come to one only from other human beings, HOPE, too, can be given to one only by other human beings."

ELIE WIESEL

Permission

It is not nice, nor is it kind to steal from people.

Please take a moment to ask me and receive written permission to copy or share any part of my book.

No one likes a copycat.

I have made a concerted effort and tried my very best to give credit to those who have taught and shared with me through their books, podcasts, interviews, videos, articles regarding healing, health and wellness.

If I have forgotten anyone, I am sincerely sorry and if brought to my attention, I will write a personal note of apology. By chance this book makes a second edition; I will gladly correct my error/s.

Medical Disclaimer

The following pages are chockfull of my experiences, my thoughts, my gentle suggestions, my opinions and most of all, my **Practical Hope**.

In no way do I think my way is the one and only correct way. I do however know it is the right way for me.

The following pages are 100% my opinions and in no way should they take the place of what your doctor or medical professional tells you.

I am not a doctor. Nor did I ever want to be one. I wanted to be a window designer for a downtown department store and a pilot. Full disclosure, I would not look good in a polyester white coat.

I take zero responsibility for anything you try from my suggestions and you become ill or damaged or don't like the outcome.

Ultimately, we are responsible for our own health or lack thereof.

Masking Tape

There is an extremely high possibility in the early morning hours of January 1969, you would have found my two sisters and I, sitting on medium shag carpeting, watching Saturday morning cartoons. We each would have been wearing our full length, long sleeved, flannel, granny gown pajamas. Sitting crisscross applesauce, lined up in order of our age; the fabric of our sleepwear would have been pulled over our knees with the hemmed edge tucked under the toes of our bare feet.

Believe it or not, our toes would have been on the edge of a piece of masking tape adhered to the variegated green carpet. Masking tape that my father had put there and my mother was not happy about. The tape on the floor was in the middle of the family room, in her very clean and organized home, the tape not looking very proper.

In attempts to not wake our parents, we would sit close to the television so the volume could be low. I think our Dad got so weary of telling us to move back from the television set on a weekly basis, that he finally just put a piece of tape on the floor and said something along the lines of, if you are watching television, you must stay behind the line.

Our very intelligent, go to work in a suit & tie while carrying a briefcase kind of father, told us that if you sat closer than 6 feet from the television set, the radiation emitted would make us sick and give us cancer (we had no idea what that was). That being said so many times, I could not possibly count, we followed the rules. Honestly, if I close my eyes for a moment, I can still "see and feel" the masking tape stuck onto the shag carpeting.

Thirty years later, you would have seen my two sisters and I dressed in proper black dresses, each of us wearing a string of pearls, standing in order of our birth, attending our father's funeral. Our Dad passed away from cancer.

His diagnosis was likely more from serious stress, smoking three packs of cigarettes daily, heavy alcohol consumption, poor food choices to list a few, than from him occasionally watching Saturday afternoon football (I never once recall my father sitting on the floor to watch television).

Looking back, in his own unique home decorator sort of way, he did indeed plant a very important seed of knowledge.

You have the ability to make many choices and those choices directly affect the outcome of your health.

Fourteen years after my father's death, I was diagnosed with cancer.

I am going to fast forward through my story and to let you know, I finally remembered what my Dad was trying to tell me.

My choices, my health outcome.

First, I had to be honest with myself. Not to be mean, judgmental or hard on myself, just a simple list. An actual, black pen to lined paper written list. A grocery list if you will, not involved and wordy, just a word or two on each line, just a place to begin. What was I doing that created this perfect storm? What could I do differently to achieve a different outcome? What was I missing? What was I doing to prevent healing from occurring?

There had to be a reason(s) how I landed in such a pot of hot water. I got myself into this, surely there were some things I could do to unravel this mess?

Our bodies can heal itself of anything if you provide it the right environment to do so.

Let the detective work begin. Some may call it research and study; I like to think of it as detective work. Goes down a little smoother, I think. Oh, please don't misunderstand. I take the work of healing very seriously. My life depends on it.

About 2 months after being diagnosed, I started the work and to this day, ten plus years later, I continue. The roll up your sleeves, set the kitchen timer, one hour a day, 5 days a week, 11 months a year work. I adore a good mystery, so the thought of being a detective to "solve" the problem is very appealing.

I will share and you will hear practical, hands on HOPE.

Hope in the form of tips and gentle suggestions, things that have worked.

If you are reading this book, you most likely have heard about and have been curious about "The List". Any time I have mentioned that I was going to write a book, the curious and polite, in some form or another, would always say, "I can't wait to read your list".

Once we began the detective work, I needed a way to track what I was doing wrong and what I did to change it.

Keeping a list and re-reading said list, actually made me feel hopeful. Keeping track of how many carrots I ate, the deodorant I changed, or the purity of the water I drank gave me hope on the days when hope seemed elusive.

It started to add up. I wrote down and numbered each thing I changed for the better. It got to be such a list; we switched to keeping track, adding and updating on a spread sheet.

Before you jump to "The List" thinking there is one magic trick, one pill, one single glorious thing you can change to heal from cancer or any other serious medical problem, let me be the first to gently as I can, disavow you of that notion.

Please take a moment to wrap your brain around that. There is no magic pill. No magic elixir. There is no magic medicine or test. The secret is YOU.

Let me be the first to give you PRACTICAL HOPE and tell you that through detective work, research, reading, I have learned that there are 450+ ways to heal from cancer. Did you hear that? Stop. Go back and read that sentence once again. Those 450+ ideas, my new friend are 450+ reasons to be hopeful!

Maybe you and your spirit are crushed? I am sincerely sorry. You are fragile & hurt right now. Maybe someone in a white coat told you the days or months left you have on your dance card. They are NOT being a decent human to another human. They are showing off and pretending to know the exact date you will perish. Bullies are meanies in sheep's clothing. They are not offering you hope and kindness. It is always hard to say no to a bully.

To the medical personnel who gave me 6 months to live, first *how dare* you play God? Second, shame on you for even thinking you have the power to tell someone their end date. What you said was cruel, mean, callous, unhelpful, and horrid. You will answer for your poor choice of words. No portion of your words fall under the heading, "Do No Harm".

To you I say, ten years later, I AM STANDING RIGHT HERE. I am going to spend my remaining days offering thoughtful, well informed, practical hope. When I am standing at the pearly gates, I am going to humbly and with gracious heart answer for my behavior.

450+ ways that may or may not jive with the mainstream, conventional, powerful, advertised and marketed way to handle this or any other disease.

Somewhere along the allopathic medical way, someone forgot to gently remind me and you what Hippocrates said,

> "The natural healing force within each of us
> is the greatest force in getting well."

Stop.

Please go back and re-read that last sentence. I will wait. Heck, go find an old tube of lipstick, after reading this book, you will likely want to toss that chemical filled lipstick or will only want to use it to write inspirational quotes on the bathroom mirror. Yes, it is that IMPORTANT, that HOPEFUL.

To you who are seriously considering taking the path less traveled, you who are curious to find the healing force within you, I say, I AM STANDING RIGHT HERE.

I am in your corner. Through this book, I will offer you HOPE in tangible ways. You are not alone. I hear you. I see you. I value you. I promise to stand with you, with my hand on your shoulder giving you support.

Together we can start to figure this out.

Good news, you do not have to wear a long flannel granny gown from Sears & Roebuck, with your bare toes touching a piece of masking tape to be happy, healthy and thriving.

In this together, new friend, here's to our Good Health!

"Hope is the only thing stronger than fear."

ROBERT LUDLUM

My Story

We all have our idiosyncrasies and reasons for them. I was raised a proper young lady and that also includes modesty in my dressing and thoughts. I was raised with specific Christian practices with strong ties to the Christian Science Church. It doesn't take a counselor to understand going for several surgeries and taking medicine in one day played havoc on my physical body and still does with my belief system.

I was 51 years old the year that this wellness journey began. Ultimately, I was diagnosed with Breast Cancer and Hypoparathyroidism.

After several appointments, each ending with a determination that it was "nothing," the doctor decided I needed a biopsy. In my ignorance, I did not know what that was.

I went to the hospital and waited. I was told what a pretty scarf I had on then ushered into the dressing room to remove all clothing and put on a backless gown. Of course, I did not feel comfortable walking anywhere in that. They said it was fine. I put on my coat. I asked if Bruce could be with me. NO! NO spouses were allowed. This is highly medical.

Then I was ushered into a dimly lit room. Take off your coat. Lay on the table and the doctor will be in shortly. Before the doctor walked in, FOUR other people came in and stood around the table. Then the doctor came in. All FOUR people had to hold my arms and legs down so the procedure could be accomplished. All he said, was, "I am Dr. somebody", you will need to hold still. He then used a gun type machine to punch a hole to remove tissue to send to the lab. He had to do it twice. The first wasn't a good enough sample.

He was done. He left. Then three of the people quietly slipped out of the room. The one nurses aid who was left, said you need to go for a mammogram now. They need to see if they got the right sample. She said just walk down the hallway. I said I needed my coat. She said no you don't. I put on my coat.

She said then you can get dressed and wait in the waiting room. After an hour wait, in tears, shocked, and stunned, someone came out, pronounced my name incorrectly, and said I could leave.

The next scheduled appointment was a date with my surgeon. I was to go for an appointment to figure out the schedule for the days and weeks ahead. Little did I know this was not completely accurate.

We were ushered into a well appointed, very large conference room. A huge 30 foot beautiful wood table in the middle with large, black leather chairs surrounding it. We sat on one side. In came three doctors in white coats. They sat on the other side: one surgeon, one oncologist, one radiologist.

I don't remember much. It was a huge power play. They were running this show. After the meeting I was told they would each examine me. So of course, that is all I could think of. Oh, I did hear them say, stop all juicing right now. You cannot have juice; the chemotherapy will not work if you do that.

Following the meeting, I was ushered into another huge room. The nurse told me to remove my clothing and lay on the table. While I was doing that, she gave Bruce some books on cancer, a pink pin and a paper that named a place where I could buy a wig.

Then each doctor took a turn and examined me. I was embarrassed. I was crushed and broken. No hope. They were in charge. I had no say in what was going on. I was a number. Like a mob hit men, they had done their job, they had killed my spirit.

We had to rush. NO time to waste. We had to move quickly. This needs to be addressed as soon as possible. Your life depends on it! Surgery was scheduled. There is no choice but to act quickly.

Side note: Not one medical person mentioned that to get to the point I was, it had taken cancer 7 to 10 years to develop this far along. Not one person said, breathe. No one gently suggested I take 30 days to calm down, think, study, learn, research, pray, gather a support system and then come to a solid, good decision.

This is an EMERGENCY! You need surgery sooner rather than later.

Surgery will be on both breasts. Cancer in one. Pre-cancer in the other. Thyroid surgery at the same time.

Side note: As you already know, I am not a doctor. Here is a gentle suggestion that it was too much at one time. I was a complete and utter mess. Too much trauma at once, it was extremely hard to recover. It never occurred to me that it was a better fit within *their* schedule. I could not think straight. I was in a fog.

After surgery, oh yes, the tingling in your feet is overwhelming. Normal. Just take some Tums. What? Problem solved.

They never discussed before or after the removal of lymph nodes. They took 4. Why? Oh, it was in the lymph nodes. No one ever said.....good news... the lymph nodes are doing what they are **SUPPOSED** to do. They find toxins and gather them and remove them from the body. Not one doctor, nurse, nurses aid, helper, not one single person explained the list of procedures they were going to do WITHOUT my clear knowledge. I was never given the grace of making an informed, clear, common sense choice.

One thing I remember, I wore a bra to the hospital and of course other clothes. They were all supposed to be waiting for me after. They were not. They could not find my $60.00 bra. The answer was, that sort of thing happens. Really? Why?

Surgery day. Does anyone actually sleep the night before surgery? The answer is no. I got up and started trying to go step by step. Nerves were winning. Shower, do my hair. The paperwork tells you not to use any products on your hair. Um, that is not going to happen. I had to use some.

Again, the paperwork said no make-up. For a girl of 50-something who has worn make up every day of her life since junior high, that is asking a lot. Then the "rules" went on to say no nail polish. Come to find out, my makeup, jewelry, nail polish, clothing, hair styling, lotions and perfumes are my set of "armor". Right or wrong, those things add up to make me who I am and give me the courage to step out into public.

Get to the hospital. Go to the place to prepare. They gave me a locker. Take off all your clothes and shoes and put on the hospital gown and ugly brown slippers with dots on the bottom. I can feel the dots through the thin material. No shoes, just those socks. Then wait in this area. I had wrapped my coat around me. Nerves and the temperature caused me to be cold and made my teeth chatter.

Thanks be to God that they allowed Bruce to be with me. I can't remember, but something tells me I was a bitch to him and scared and nervous and said horrid mean things. I am sincerely sorry. I was just so scared.

I waited over an hour like that. It felt like they were breaking me down on purpose. Of course, their schedule was all goofy and they did not have a smooth set up.

I was then told to go to the next office. I had been told about this before. It was on my mind. I had to walk through the hospital in a hospital gown, no make-up, no jewelry, and no shoes. I wrapped my long winter coat around me for some modesty and protection. Again, I had to check in. Do you have ID? Bruce took care of that. I was mean and angry and scared and nervous. Go wait in the waiting room with other people. I sat in a room, with just a hospital gown on and socks, no makeup and I felt crushed. It was about to get worse.

My name was called. Pronounced wrong, of course. Ushered into a medical procedure room. Two people.

They knew ahead of time what was going to happen. They told me it was going to hurt.

The procedure was Barbaric. (As an afterthought, this seems like a procedure that could have better been handled once they put me to sleep for the surgery. I look back now and think how animalistic it was. It was full power for them. They, in one fell swoop, striped me of any dignity I may have had) Honestly, the worst, most degrading, painful procedure of my life.

No anesthesia, they proceeded to thread a wire through my breast to the certain point where the tumor was. It stung like a son of a bitch. They moved, pulled, wiggled, and pushed. (I think Bruce was holding my hand.) It was the worst possible moment of my life. That hurt worse than anything I have been through. I tried closing my eyes. It didn't help. Then it got worse. They had to do it all over again on the other breast. Hold me down while they did this. Then with the wire sticking out and rubbing against my hospital gown, okay, you are done. Walk back over to the surgery room. You will then be prepped for surgery.

Primum Non Nocere

"Do no harm" is thought to be part of the original ancient Greek Hippocratic oath.

Although the phrase does not appear in the AD 245 version of the oath, similar intentions are vowed "I will abstain from all intentional wrong-doing and harm."

In 1973, the US Supreme Court rejected the oath as a guide to medical ethics.

I went to stand up. I was woozy. I was weak. It was the first time in my life that I actually hated other human beings.

I am aware that some folks love the attention of surgery and medical procedures. I am not one of those people. I had been broken. So there I was: scared to death, cold, no makeup, no jewelry, no clothing, in pain, nervous. I am guessing that my immune system that was not properly working before just hit an all-time low in my life. Now, I had to wrap my brain around going for surgery and medicine that my religion has said is not okay. It was simply the lowest I had ever felt. I got up onto the surgical bed and had to say good bye to Bruce. The one touchstone I had.

The first time in my life, that I felt "they" had won. They scared me into thinking I needed this surgery. They didn't teach or guide or suggest any type of research on my own. This was hurry up, you need this. You must do this.

Again, it is hard to say no to bullies.

Gosh, if this truly was a deadly disease, and I was going to die from it, it was sure a taste of the end. Not one thing was kind or humane about this. Pure agony. Here I am 10 plus years later still thinking about it now and then. Still hurt by it. Still not liking people or hospitals or hospital workers.

Maybe people need to hear how horrid humans can be to other humans?

I felt striped of all personal power I ever foolishly thought I had. I guess they have to be business-like and get people through the schedule. I was not even treated with kindness. I was nothing to them.

If I had to go back and look them in the eye, I would say, you won. You broke me down. You won.

Years later, I have to wonder, if possibly there were some things that could have gone smoother. I guess, by that point I was a number. I was someone with surgical needs that would make the hospital over $500,000.00. By the time the cancer train has left the station, it is moving forward and you feel as though you do not have the ability or the choice to stop it.

The checkup 6 weeks later was to tell me they didn't do their job well enough and didn't "get it all". So, I would have to do it ALL OVER again. *Oh, we just happen to have an open surgery time for tomorrow!* By that point, I didn't care. They had won.

Despite having to wear an ugly red plastic hospital bracelet and a huge, ugly red sign above my hospital bed stating that I have an allergy to MSG, I was unable to eat 95% of the food (it contained MSG) offered in the hospital. In addition to sleeping in my room and never leaving me except to get food, Bruce brought me Miso soup and fruit for all meals.

When I hear from so many people that have been diagnosed with cancer, surgery is needed because theirs is a "unique", "rare" cancer and the surgeons have to "act fast." Then comes "we didn't get it all". Wow, if I was to compose a thesis, this would be an interesting topic. Prescribe surgery, not get it all and have to do more surgery and guess what? Bill the insurance company for two surgeries every single time, certainly a brilliant money maker. The patient is scared out of their wits, they are armed with their lowest amount of courage to stand up and then the medical professionals say, you need to have another surgery. Like a zombie, the patients answers okay, do whatever.

Now that I have typed all that, I thought it would leave my memory bank and I would feel 100 pounds lighter. I don't. However, I am trying to move forward by writing these words and leave them here. Needless to say, as I type I have on two shirts. Not a day has gone by since that surgery that I don't think of cancer. Not a day goes by that I don't wear modest clothing. I wear make up every single day. I wear jewelry every single day. I still don't like being out of control. I don't like being chilled to the bone for hours on end.

I am making some progress in the mental health department of my life. Just two weeks ago, I donated my beautiful, very expensive, long winter wool coat. I no longer want to be reminded of the day that I wore that coat as my armor.

The surgeries were done. The medical establishment left me with a damaged immune system. I was left unable to keep my balance - both physically and emotionally. Unless I wanted to go through more surgery, I was left disfigured and deformed and in pain. Another hit on my mental health and well being. Not one word was uttered as to what food to eat, what actions to take to help heal.

It was about 6 weeks after the second surgery. We had our appointment with the oncologist. While in the waiting room, I picked up a brochure, *Naturopath and Cancer.*

I was raised with a strict belief system about medicine and healing. I thought maybe the brochure would be of some help to me. At least it could be a starting point to choose a different path. Somehow during the appointment, I managed to inquire about the brochure. He asked where I had gotten that. I said in your waiting room. He dismissed it. Maybe if I was true to myself, and could remember exactly, that might have been the spark of a moment. I have this slip of glossy paper in my hand and he questioned me. Like a small puppy....oh, I have something they don't want me to have. . I grasped the paper tighter than ever.

To say I was struggling mightily with my imbedded belief system with medical appointments and procedures and surgeries would be a humongous understatement.

The oncologist had designed his very well-appointed office to convey the type of person he wished he was. He had a very impressive array of Catholic symbols, religious books and several framed certificates. His polyester white coat pressed with his name embroidered over the pocket. He would be deflated to know; I do not remember his name. I have never once tried to remember it. I ask Bruce not to repeat the name. It is less than necessary for me to give it or him any credence.

It was all for show. The office was designed to present an illusion of intelligence and of a faithful person, calculated and done on purpose. It was to create an illusion of Power, Intimidation and Control.

I don't remember every single detail.

I do remember him saying he was prescribing chemotherapy and radiation. He said I would need to take Tamoxifen for five years.

A random thought popped into my head. I timidly asked, "I have heard that Tamoxifen will give you cancer?" He answered directly and quickly. "Yes, but we can address that when it happens."

*Side Note: *Tamoxifen is classified by the World health organization and the American Cancer Society as a human carcinogen. It has been documented to cause over two-dozen health-destroying side effects, yet it is still used as a first-line treatment for certain types of breast cancer.*

"One of the first duties of the physician is to educate the masses not to take medicine."

WILLIAM OSLER (1849 – 1919) DESCRIBED AS THE FATHER OF MODERN MEDICINE

Here is a thought to ponder: hospitals and oncology clinics, and oncologists themselves buy cancer drugs at wholesale prices then mark them up and sell them to you. Making a legal profit to which the conflict of interest is quite simply mind boggling.

Did you know that chemotherapy "cures" breast cancer 2.8% of the time? That means the people who have chosen that path and have lived are indeed angels among us. They have walk over the hot coals and survived long term. I tip my hat to them and their courage.

I remember my hands sweating and I was shaking. I remember going into my head. I had all but stopped listening to him at this point. Somehow, I did work up the courage, out of the blue, I asked quietly, "What about me getting a second opinion?" He said, well, I guess my colleague can give you one.

Really? The person for whom you write their annual reviews and who works for you will give me a different, educated, non-biased opinion?

This is similar to a doctor ordering a bevy of diagnostic testing from the exact same institution that will profit from all the suggested procedures and surgeries.

He did ask if we were still vegetarians. I said yes. He said, "You may as well eat dirt".

For the insurance to pay, I needed a referral from him. He was not happy.

He was writing the referral and Bruce and I were talking quietly. At one point, he told us to be quiet.

Every ounce of energy I had was coursing through my fingers. I could feel the wooden arms of the chair. I am sure there was more conversation. I can't honestly remember nor could I hear him. He didn't know it, however, I did. I was done.

This was the moment. Courage was tapping me on the shoulder. My gut was turning and bubbling and growling and trying to somehow get my attention. The hair on the back of my neck was standing up.

Believe it or not, it was not a huge yelling, loud, bravado moment. It was extremely quiet. I was polite and to the point.

I said, no thank you.

I gripped the arms of the chair; I pushed with all my strength to stand up.

As I placed both hands on either side of me, I felt the smooth slender arms of an office chair. I stood up; I looked him in the eyes and said, no thank you.

It has been ingrained in my very being to offer a handshake for someone's time, civilized pleasantries. I did not.

I looked down. That would be the last time I looked into someone's eyes for several days.

I glanced down and focused on my polished Leather Penny Loafers. They are brown with a hint of deep Burgundy color. I can see the even stitches with heavy duty thread that was used to sew them together. I can see a scuff mark on the top of the right foot. Each shoe has a penny tucked into the small leather flap. I took a step, then another. It was an even cadence. I could feel the floor through the sole of each foot.

In the background, I could hear Bruce saying something to the doctor. Almost immediately, behind me, I could hear his footsteps. I could feel his presence.

Trying to untangle myself from the halls and levels of the hospital, we were silent. Riding the elevator down, I remained silent. As, I step out of the elevator, I was fixated on my loafers. I kept walking. The atrium was huge. From previous visits, I knew that the domed ceiling was beautiful, no need to look up. My feet somehow propelled me forward toward the door. For some reason, I didn't choose the revolving door. Off to the side was a single door. I stopped in front of it and could feel Bruce's arm reach out to push it open. The cooler, outdoor fresh air whooshed over my face. I felt a chill. I kept standing and walking forward. I could feel people around me, seeing their shape, but not looking at anyone directly. The parking lot was humungous and cars filled the slots. Bruce somehow guided me down the correct isle.

The tears started dropping out of my eyes. No sound, just drops of tears spotting my clothing and some on my loafers.

We got to the car. He opened my door and I got in. I said, what am I going to do? Bruce said "I love you, WE will figure this out together. WE can do it."

I was diagnosed with Breast Cancer & Hypoparathyroidism.

Several appointments later....getting set up for the schedule, tattoo dots for radiation, "you can never miss a day". Well no, we are not open on Saturday and Sundays or holidays. We don't do treatment on those days. However, you cannot miss a day. The schedule is not tailor made for each person, each condition, and each variation. There is a treatment duration and it is set in stone.

I was in the middle of making my decision. I was slow to respond to inquiries. I was dragging my feet and if I listened to my belief system and walked away, I was trying to figure out what was available to me. How would I look myself in the mirror if I jumped ship on my actual beliefs?

Side Note:

In America, if you are Jewish you are not required to work on your Sabbath, nor are you asked to remove your yamaka in the work place or business. If you are Amish, you are not required to have electricity or buy a car. If you are of Islamic faith, no one would require you to join them in a weekend of gambling and drinking alcohol.

However, if your religious faith is the Christian Science denomination that guides you away from traditional medicine, then you are up a creek. You are on your own to figure out how to heal. You are not given any other option than that of main stream allopathic medicine. *You are ridiculed.* You are called names. You are dismissed. Hearing from others that you should forgo your religion for the welfare and benefit of others, hurts my soul. Hearing someone say that my choice is ridiculous and I should just go along to get along and not cause waves, doesn't sit well with me.

By treating me "less than" because of my belief system is not kind. By being mean and nasty because I do not conform to your way of thinking is a poor way to treat another human being.

The phone calls and emails started coming fast and furious. They berated Bruce every day, several times a day. He needed to make me understand. They needed me to start immediately. Why was I being stubborn? He needed to convince me. They even called Bruce at his job. The calls were to get Bruce to get me to start chemotherapy on the day they had scheduled and radiation to follow. Why was I being hard headed? I needed to follow through and do what they said.

We even went so far as to tour the medical building where the chemotherapy would take place. I remember in the waiting area there was a huge, empty container, with black sharpie marker writing on the outside. It read SUGAR. It was in the coffee area. The workers who administered the poisonous chemotherapy were dressed head to toe in hazmat suits. Needless to say, as I walked out of the beautiful building, my mind was swirling.

Days later, I was in our backyard raking leaves. Yet another phone call came to Bruce. He came out and said the radiologist wants an answer.

I said, no, thank you. I went back to raking leaves.

The following is the story of how I managed to stay afloat after the doctor told Bruce, that if I did not do Chemotherapy and Radiation, I would not see Christmas, probably less than 6 months to live..............I am alive 10 plus years later (yes, on any given day, I know the exact year, month and day).

I am standing right here.

My goal of writing this book is to change the narrative in my life.

I no longer want to live in heartache, gloom, anguish and hate.

I chose to write my story and share solutions and gentle suggestions.

I made up this fictitious woman to whom I am writing. In my mind, she lives in Iowa. While waiting to pick up her kids from school, she is wondering along a sidewalk sale, mind swirling. She sees my book, flips through the pages. It is for sale on the $1.00 table. She buys it.

...and that is how the story begins.

I want to give her kindness in the form of **Practical Hope**.

Why me?

The days, weeks and months following hearing the words "You have cancer," I asked, shouted, cried, screamed, swore, prayed on bended knee, and begged the question to God and to the universe "why me?" I asked so many times I got tired of asking.

I don't know about you, however, one of my biggest and first questions was.....Why me? Take a deep breath; take one more before you read my answer.

After years of research, detective work, swirling ideas, asking questions, one of my favorite answers came from Ryan Holiday, he has helped me in answering the "why" question. It may not speak to you, however, please, give it a chance. Read what he has to share. Reread it two weeks from now, two years and 3 months from now.... (See what I did there? I gave you hope! Oh yes, you and I will be around two years and three months from now to discuss this idea once again).

Ryan Holiday teaches about Marcus Aurelius. In his list of 9 rules for a better life, he gives us all a clear cut answer, albeit in Latin.

Amor Fati
"It didn't happen <u>to</u> you. It happened <u>for</u> you.
Fate chose this for you. Accept it. Embrace it. Bear it. Make something of it.
A fire turns everything into fuel and brightness, that's Amor Fati."

Many different studies have shown up to 95% of cancers are caused by diet, lifestyle and environmental factors.

If you get out your calculator and do the math, this means that it is more than likely that you did not get breast cancer because your grandpa had lung cancer.

If you really want to not just survive but thrive in health and wellness, then maybe you need to figure out the puzzle. By putting on your detective hat, there is a good to better chance that you will be able to remove the problems and get on with a healthy life.

I made a list of several things, some were easy to fix, and other items took months to repair and others I needed to save up for. To name a few on my list:

Estrogen and Estrogen mimickers

A lack of quality bio-available supplements and minerals

Poor quality Water

Stress

Unresolved forgiveness issues

Diet Coke

Poor sleep

Too much sugar, dairy, white flour

Antibiotics from recent surgery

Artificial food coloring

Dental issues

Lack of sunshine

Not enough exercise

Poor Food choices

Plastics

Parasites

You have to make your own list. You have to be brutally honest. No, making a list is not to beat yourself up, rather to enlighten you and get you on a new path of health and healing. That way you can address each issue. If you really want to heal and regain wellness, you have to know what you need to change.

Hey, by the way, has the doctor you are seeing asked you how you got cancer? If you don't know how it happened, how will any of us know how to correct the issue?

Gentle Suggestion

Make a list.

Start tackling the list so you can regain your health and vitality.

Your Angel is Whispering, are You Listening?

When I was a little girl, my dad drove a couple hours away to pick up my Grandma Hazel and bring her to our home. She needed to spend the night so she could catch an early morning train. I didn't hear all of the discussion, but boy howdy the adults were ignoring the kids and trying to map out all the timing and such. In the morning, we all excitedly piled into the car. My sisters and I were excited to see the station and the train. My grandma didn't drive, so she had purchased a ticket to travel to another state to visit our cousins.

The train station was bustling with activity.

Her train was ready to go, over the loud speaker; the deep voice notified all the passengers that it was time to board. It was loud, exciting and everyone was moving about with hats, coats, suitcases. Everyone was hugging and saying goodbye. For us to have a better view and to wave goodbye to our grandma, my mother ushered my sisters and I closer to the train platform. Passengers were boarding and men were helping people lift and stow their suitcases. We couldn't see our grandma. Where was she?

In all the confusion, excitement, and noise, we didn't realize she was standing right next to us. She was holding her purse. My father was holding her suitcase and he looked mad. My grandmother had announced that she was not getting on the train. (To find out why she did not get on the train, read to the end of this chapter.)

Wow. What? She didn't want to take a train trip? She had made up her mind and there was nothing my mother or father said could change her mind. My sisters and I were silent. As you can imagine, the car ride home was eerily quiet.

You know "that" feeling you get on the back of your neck? Or maybe its goose bumps on your arms? What about that moment when your gut is trying to tell you something? That is called intuition; some refer to it as our sixth sense. Your

Pineal gland or Third eye is trying to get your attention. Many spiritual traditions believe it serves as a connection between the physical and spiritual worlds.

Your angel is tapping you on the shoulder and gently nudging you to use your intuition. Some folks call it the Spirit of God.

We were all given this instinctual sense of what is right for each of us. It was built into us to help keep our species alive and thriving. When something smells fishy or sounds just plain ridiculous, **listen** to your inner self. Even if you don't have all the details and it still sounds wrong, it most likely is. There is no game show music counting down the minutes you have. Step away, breathe, and give yourself the grace to think things through.

> *"Intuition is always right in at least two important ways; It is always in response to something. It always has your best interest at heart."*

GAVIN DEBECKER

Yes, you have the freedom and God given right to take a few moments or days to make an informed, thoughtful decision. This is what is referred to as Free Will.

One question I repeatedly am asked, how did you have the courage to walk away?

When I was told I would need chemotherapy and radiation, my hands started sweating, my ears were ringing and something in my stomach felt weird. I had little to no knowledge what I was going to do. Their offered "solution" sounded wrong to me.

> *"Good instincts usually tell you what to do before your head has figured it out."*

MICHAEL BURKE

The hair on the back of my neck was standing up.

The doctor was mad. I could see it in his face. I could feel the anger coming from him. I stood up and said no, thank you. The doctor was talking louder and louder and I just kept walking away.

"Focus on your healing; outside things will blur your vision."

A. CRAFT

Ps. About an hour down the tracks, the train my grandmother was scheduled to be on... derailed.

Gentle Suggestion

Listen to your inner being.

Listen to your heart & hunches.

You are of value. You are worthy of health and wellness.

This is where Free Will comes in.

Food Glorious Food

"Let Food be thy Medicine and medicine be thy food"

HIPPOCRATES

Though thousands of years old, the above quote acknowledges the importance of healthy eating and how the nutrients in various foods have healing properties.

My body understands and recognizes real food. It does not understand additives, food colorings, chemicals to make the food more salty, sweeter or shelf stable.

We were all designed to eat and process real food.

"Food is medicine. We can break the cycle of disease."

DR. JUDY MIKOVITS

One of the angels among us is Patrick Quillin, PhD, RD, CNS. He wrote the book, Beating Cancer with Nutrition. I have not only learned much from this incredibly brilliant human, I have learned you can heal using a gentle, calm, kind, graceful way. He shared, "The human body is built from, repaired by, and fueled by substances found in the diet. In the most literal sense, "we are what we eat... think, breathe, and do."

We are asked oodles of times, what do you eat?

We eat a plant rich, nutrient-dense diet. That means, in addition to plants, vegetables, fruits, legumes, nuts and seeds, on occasion, we will eat wild caught fish, and now and then organic or grass fed meat.

Years ago we hosted a graduation party. At that time, our youngest son was a vegan. I made myself a crazy girl by making vegan gravy and non-vegan gravy. I made vegan dishes and non-vegan dishes. I whipped up vegan desserts and non-vegan

35

desserts...you get the idea. I put pretty little signs near all the dishes to designate which food was what.

Later that night, at 1:00 am, while doing dishes, I told Mr. Right, stick a fork in me, I am DONE.

While cleaning up from the party and doing *twice* as many dishes as normal, I decided to make some changes.

NASA had a mission statement, "Get there". I needed a mission statement.

My new mission statement:

Make/bake/share excellent quality healthy food with exceptional taste.

I wanted my food to be so good that I don't have to put a sign on it to qualify what it is. I don't want to say: this is dairy-free or gluten-free or sugar-free. I don't have to say, these crab cakes are made with Jack Fruit (no actual crab). I don't have to explain this is vegetarian or vegan. I decided to make and share exceptional healthy food.

When you come to my house and enjoy a Chocolate Chip Cookie, I won't be explaining that they are dairy-free, gluten-free, sugar-free...blah, blah, blah. You will just ask for another.

If you try my chicken nuggets, I will not be telling you that there is no chicken involved. Nor will I explain that my donuts are non-dairy and gluten free.

I will share a list of foods that have helped me heal; you might find different foods to add to your own list. I was reading and learning as fast as I could, especially foods that would build my immunity and help stop cancer growth. Eating real whole food is a brilliant way to address *all* major diseases and aliments. I do encourage you to keep a list. It feels pretty darn powerful when you look back at the list of foods you have tried to help your body do what it was designed to do.

Fun fact: we looked up how much our car weighed, then celebrated when we juiced that many carrots! That's a lot of "medicine". That's a whole lot of healing.

Here is a thought to ponder: what you are currently doing is apparently not working. If you have any kind of aliment you might consider having a look at what you are eating.

While some whole foods are delicious and beautiful and taste wonderful, some are the opposite to me. I still gave it a go. Not everything is going to be to your liking. Sometimes, you gotta put on your kick-ass red cowgirl boots and "get 'er done".

Here are a couple of unappetizing things I tried after I learned the positive effects in healing disease. I ate one organic radish daily for 90 days. I took a small one to begin with, I chewed fast and swallowed. For an entire year, I drank a 6 ounce cup of Chaga Tea (which to me, tasted like dirt) by plugging my nose and drinking fast. When I ground up fresh organic lemons with the peel and a head of raw garlic in filtered water I didn't go slowly, I forged ahead, plugged my nose and drank it. Done. Have a drink of water, clean up the dishes, and move on.

Keep an open mind, stay curious, and try shopping at a Mexican or Asian grocery store. We have found that international markets offer a much larger, varied selection of fresh, wholesome produce.

One note about cooking and or heating food. No microwave. Throw it out. **"Microwave safe, means the container, not your health."**

The following is a list of some amazingly powerful "get well" and stay well foods.

"You are what you eat, so don't be fast, cheap, easy, or fake."

UNKNOWN AUTHOR

Whole foods (non-GMO and organic if possible)

Turmeric: We use raw in our juicing. Also available
in dried. Easy to add while cooking

Green Tea: Make an effort to find green tea that does not contain lead.

Cruciferous vegetables

Fermented food & drinks

Figs: reduces inflammation, anti oxidant, detoxs the colon

Chaga: most immune nourishing substance on earth. www.Birchboys.com

Broccoli sprouts: 18 times more powerful that full grown Broccoli

Sprouts

Cinnamon

Raw honey, Bee Pollen

All berries

Black Raspberries: 99% grown in Oregon, www.BerriHealth.com

Chili peppers

Herbs

Eat cooked mushrooms

Healthy fats – avocado, nuts, fish, seeds

Pomegranates: royal fruit, 613 seeds, (613 laws
of the Bible), can cause apoptosis

Green mangos

Lemon: Juice, flesh and peel (organic)

Garlic: eat as much as you can as often as you can. Please check that
it was grown in the USA, or better yet grow some yourself.

Gentle Suggestion

Eat real food.

Road Trip

Everyone loves a road trip. With a day or two notice or a month ahead, the anticipation is glorious. The time in the car to talk, the snacks, the sightseeing, it all adds up to something new and wonderful.

Weather your map is marked for a day trip to the Olympic Peninsula to see the largest Western Red Cedar tree in the world, Jake the Alligator Man (alleged half-man, half-alligator, at Marsh's Free Museum), or a slightly longer road trip to the Sea Lion Caves in Florence, Oregon, any road trip is most certainly going to involve food.

We started taking Sunday drives to relax, escape the pressure of learning to heal and forget about any new healthy lifestyle switcharoos. After a few hours, I was hungry and there was not a fast food place in the land that offered food I was able to eat. I will spare you the details of the frustrations, grumpy attitude and crying meltdowns.

I will admit to being a bit jelly of all the cars lined up at restaurants. They would stay in their car, speak into a box, pull around the building, hand over some money and pull ahead to the window. Some cheerful employee would pass out a paper bag with food and drinks. Easy peasy.

Sometimes we tried to choose more upscale eateries thinking we could get something to eat. Please not one more plain baked potato or heaven help me, no thank you to: our "healthy" option is Butternut Squash stuffed ravioli.

When we were near a larger town, we stopped at a grocery store to forage for a banana, hummus, some "healthy" snacks. It was sad, pathetic and did not fill our bellies.

Then if we just ate a little something to hold us over until home, once home, we needed to come up with some amazing satisfying healthy food for a meal. Yes ma'am, please have dinner planned and waiting in your refrigerator before you head out on a day trip. You will secretly thank me for that tip. You're welcome.

Next order of business for us…road tripping got a remake, a reboot, a do-over! This is what I would share with a friend, asking for road trip food suggestions. You may already surmise that I have a lot practical hope for amazing on the road, food.

First and foremost, invest in an updated, excellent quality cooler. Believe me, the one you have been using is 31 years old and technology has come a long way. Save up, you and your future glorious, unbelievable, delicious, well appointed picnics will be all the better for it. If you are more into day hikes, you might consider looking into the backpacks that have cooler capabilities.

Next up the actual picnic basket needs an overhaul. An old shopping bag or card board box to toss things into is not what I am talking about. I am sharing about a honest to goodness well-made picnic basket, back pack, soft sided tote, whatever works for you. If you received a "romantic" fully stocked picnic basket as a shower gift, now is the time to get it out of the guest room closet and put it to good use.

Planning ahead will make you feel happy, over and over and over. You only have to do this once, and then you are ready to hit the road. Make the effort, you are worth it. The following are items for you to consider as you pack your take along bag, always packed (and refilled), so that with a days notice you can easily grab and go.

You are worth the real thing. Let me explain:

I purchased some plates that actually look like paper plates; however, they are made of Corelle. They always make me giggle and they are non-breakable. There is a whole host of patterns and choices; surely you will find something that you love. I have found kits already made up in the camping area of sporting goods stores that include plates, silverware, cups etc. for travel. Everyone has enough real silverware with extra pieces to use, pack enough for you and your families to each have a genuine knife, fork and spoon. We prefer cloth napkins. However sometimes, those amazing sammies you create are drippy and require a few paper napkins. Of course you will need cups, glasses, tumblers with lids or even a snazzy glass bottle.

Once you get those things gathered, it's time to fill up your essentials bag. I sewed one out of adventure travel fabric; however, you can find already premade bags that would work perfectly. Fill it up with travel salt and pepper, a bottle opener, cork screw, birthday candles, matches, wet wipes (if you use those, or like me have a baggie ready to toss in a wet washcloth with a splash of white vinegar from home), toothpicks, clips to close bags, a roll of tape, small travel scissors, a small knife and so forth. Having items on hand and ready will be super useful for the trip.

Also consider a picnic blanket that rolls up very neatly. One side is material with a waterproof coating. It is perfect for on the ground, or in a pinch the tablecloth. Some of the picnic baskets you can purchase come with this type of blanket.

Okay, now on to the good stuff, food glorious food.

As you have probably guessed by now, I make about 90% of all our food, sauces, condiments etc. You do not need to. I just like knowing all the ingredients and as a side hobby I enjoy cooking and baking. Depending on where you live, you might check with your local delicatessen, bakery; some caterers will sell boxed lunches or try the deli counter at your grocery store. Have I mentioned I make an amazing maple syrup and mustard dipping sauce? www.itdoesnttastelikechicken.com

Remember that feeling of being a bit jelly of the cars lined up getting food fast? Your mission is to satiate your appetite and have really amazing, flavorful, lush, satisfying, leaning towards gourmet food. The trick here is to fill your basket with ready, available and far superior choices that anything you can get at a drive thru fast food establishment. You need to feel happy and proud of your food selections and you are looking forward with anticipation to an amazing meal.

Maybe pack things that you feel are a treat, same goes for drinks. Yes, you will have your filtered water; however, this might be a great time to treat yourself to a real fruit Kombucha. Have you considered a store-bought organic juice or a sparkling cider you have wanted to try?

Keep a list of items you have made or purchased that work really well. That way each outing you won't have to reinvent the wheel, or if you are not in a creative mood, don't feel inspired, you can glance back at things you have already enjoyed and would like to have again.

Because you are not limited to what is printed on the fast food menu, the world is your oyster! You have unlimited possibilities of real food, that you actually like and will feel downright happy to indulge in.

Chef salads or jar salads toppings might include, cooked wild caught salmon, grass fed beef, cooked and sliced paper thin, *nitrate free* deli turkey

Extra large gourmet olives

"Chicken" salad sammies

Crepes to fill with cut up strawberries

Fancy pretzels

Homemade peanut butter (you already bought a juicer, toss in some peanuts, magically you just made peanut butter)

Make or buy some calzones

Potato salad

Figs

Biscuits, coconut whipped cream and sliced strawberries

Hard boiled eggs

Seasonal berries

Cut up watermelon and tuck in a couple toothpicks to use as "utensils"

Hummus and crackers

Falafel, sauce, cucumbers and pita bread

Israeli couscous salad

Niçoise salad

Caprese sandwich or salad

Cashews, pecans, walnuts, pistachios

Chocolate chip cookies (the recipe I use and highly recommend is from www.theVegan8.com)

Maybe you stumble upon a highly recommended restaurant that offers real food choices? Nothing says you have to eat what you packed. (Save it for your dinner, once you are home) Another good idea is to purchase a travel book that lists plant based or healthy option restaurants in cities you will be traveling through. We have found that if you are not in a picnic mood, or just want to try a new place, having a guide book quickly opens up more options.

People often ask me where I get all my recipes, what are my favorite authors on food, blogs, books, food suggestions and so forth. I will use some of my tried and true oldies which I have elevated and replaced with healthier ingredients.

The following is list of the books that I refer to over and over. These are the books I highly recommend to friends and family. The pages in these "go-to" books are covered in notes, gold star stickers, are highlighted, have dog eared pages, oodles of smiley faces, and lots of food spills.

Since there are so many beautiful choices in the cookbook genre, before I purchase a cookbook, if my library has the book I am interested in, I check it out, try a few recipes, maybe even check it out twice, take it for a test run, then if I like it, I will buy the book.

All of the following authors also have a social media presence and are gracious in sharing all kinds of recipes. Please consider taking your time to look into their blogs, podcasts, you tube videos.

Be a Plant Based Woman Warrior, Live Fierce, Stay Bold, Eat Delicious by Jane and Ann Esselstyn
www.janeesselstyn.com

Beat Cancer Kitchen by Chris and Micah Wark
www.chrisbeatcancer.com

Crazy Sexy Kitchen by Kris Carr
www.kriscarr.com

Cultured Food for Life by Donna Schwenk
www.culturedfoodlife.com

Forks over Knives, Cookbook by Del Sroufe
www.forksoverknives.com

Fuss Free Vegan 101 by Sam Turnbull
www.itdoesnttastelikechicken.com

Happy Herbivore by Lindsay Nixon
www.happyherbivore.com

Milling Your Own Flour with Felicia
www.gritsandgrain.com

Love & Lemons, Feel Good Food by Jeanine Donofrio
www.loveandlemons.com

Love Real Food by Kathryn Taylor
www.cookiesandkate.com

One-Hour Dairy free Cheese by Claudia Lucero

Super Juicing by Tonia Reinhard

The Vegan8 by Brandi Doming
www.thevegan8.com

Gentle Suggestion

"Every time you eat or drink you are either feeding disease or fighting it."

HEATHER MORGAN

Rescue Yourself

Through my needlework hobby, I recently met a new friend. When I told her my name, she was the first person in 59 years to describe it quite like she did. *"Daleen sounds like a princess who rescues herself."*

In some magical, kind, twisted comment..............her simple statement instantly changed all my wasted time thinking about my name.

I have spent an amazing amount of time fussing over my name. My parents combined my father's name, Dale and my mother's middle name Lee. Imagine the time wasted explaining my name then waiting for the person to say it incorrectly. Over the years, I have received junk mail, legal documents, personal notes, letters, emails, texts etc. All with my name misspelled.

Think of all the time you have "wasted" waiting for a medical appointment? All while you are living life the same way, making the same poor choices that got you in this predicament. How many times you have calculated the months left before your next medical test? Stop wasting time!

You thought that by you telling your boss you have a medical appointment and need time off, you were taking action. By you telling your friends you have a medical appointment next week, or by you sharing on social media your condition, you thought you were actually doing something.

No, by taking action, I mean investing in YOU. Put on your detective hat, read a book and learn about your concerns, illness, and issues. Before you go to your next medical appointment, fill up a couple 3 X 5 cards with questions. Set that kitchen timer for one hour and learn, investigate, be curious, keep an open mind, take notes, learn. YOU are of value and this exercise is about helping and healing YOU.

The person who knows the medical answer is going to fit you into their schedule, charge you a fee and they are going to tell you what you have and how to medicate it. You have been waiting for the easiest way to "fix" the problem. Just think of all the interrupted sleep, wasted time, fretting, and waiting for the name of what you have to be bestowed upon you.

During your "waiting period" think of all the research you could fit in? You could spend every single moment of free time, learning about you and your health. Books, published papers, blogs, videos, master classes, health series, pod casts, Ted Talks and more. You could be actually doing something, taking action to answer your questions.

A couple months after my diagnosis, I needed, craved some answers. I began to read, explore, study, learn, research. It seemed rather old fashioned, however, I set the old kitchen timer for one hour. I sat at the kitchen table, put on my Deerstalker hat, (more than likely actually a baseball hat that has the words "Be Kind" on the front), and opened a book.

"My people are destroyed by the lack of knowledge"

HOSEA 4:6

I ventured onto the computer next. I am well aware that many people say there are plenty of quacks, charlatans and snake oil salesmen on the internet. Let me be the first to tell you, along with some undereducated tricksters, there happen to be some brilliant, well educated, intelligent, well learned humans who are more than willing to share the knowledge they have collected and help you on your healing journey. It might just be their calling to help others heal.

My first order of business was to dig deep and figure out who the person was that I wanted to learn from. If the person sold a book or product, that was fine. If the person took money from a large company, then I had to decide if I wanted what they were "selling".

I took daily notes. I highlighted books. I dog eared pages. Each night during dinner I would share with Mr. Right what I had learned.

That was how the 1 hour a day, 5 days a week, 11 months a year study time, became a habit, one book after another, one pod cast, and one published paper after the next.

I continue today.

This very morning, before I did some writing, I started my day with studying.

Today, I was learning a new to me idea about the healing properties of nicotine. Aww, got your attention, didn't I? Dr. Bryan Ardis is an extremely knowledgeable human and I have much to learn from him. It began with, "every single virus, flu, measles etc. targets nicotine receptors...that is how they make you sick." When he mentioned studies showing how nicotine is stopping cancer growth and Parkinson's...THAT grabbed my attention and with that ... I tumbled down the rabbit hole.

Every single day that I sit down to learn, could quite possibly be "the" day that I rescue myself.

> ## "Think for yourself, or others will think for you, without thinking of you."
>
> HENRY DAVID THOREAU

You and your good health are completely up to you.

Gentle Suggestion:

Use your time wisely.

Read, Learn and

Rescue Yourself.

Courage in a Jar

I am one fortunate, grateful, lucky girl.

I have an amazing "boyfriend" (aka, husband) with whom I have been hanging out with for 41 plus years. He is my anchor, safe place, constant, rock, safety net, steadiness, shelter. He is sturdy, loyal, intelligent, strong, funny, kind and makes one heck of a good breakfast. He is the love of my life and my Saving Grace.

But wait; there is one another man in my life. You might have heard of him, "The Duke". He seems like someone who could handle just about anything. I sort of imagine that he could and would fix most problems. I love this quote by none other than John Wayne,

"Courage is being scared to death, but saddling up anyway."

One solution of practical hope that I might offer is, buy a juicer. Buy what you can afford while saving up for a better model. Juicing vegetables and fruits and drinking that juice, has most assuredly saved my life. In the next chapter, Mr. Right will explain all about it, but for now, I just wanted to talk about how much I look forward to my beautiful, healing morning juice.

In addition to all the fine qualities that I listed about Mr. Right, there is one more. He makes our juice. Mr. Right makes juice on a nightly basis. There are Mason jars, with lids on tight, waiting every single morning, on the top shelf of our refrigerator. Yes, he even makes extra before he goes away on business trips.

Each morning, with sleepy eyes, I grab my jar and give it a rock and roll shake and I am ready to rumble. It tastes like sunshine in a jar. It is my very own glass of courage.

Giddy up, daylight is burning!

Here is the recipe: (all scrubbed clean with vinegar and rinsed with water) four carrots, two peeled oranges, one peeled lemon, one red pepper, 1 inch piece of peeled Turmeric root. Toss them all into the juicer and the magical elixir will come out all golden, glowing, vibrant orange and healthy.

For all you number freaks out there (I adore this part, so I guess that makes me a number freak) over the course of 10 plus years, that equates to approximately:

4,914 oranges

13,140 carrots

3, 276 red peppers

3,276 lemons

And a WHOLE lot of Turmeric root

That is a tremendous amount of courage and healing in one pint size Mason jar!

Tighten that belt on your fluffy, white, cozy bathrobe, turn up the music; raise your glass in a toast to you.

Say Grace and for the love of finding courage and wellness in a Mason jar; drink deeply friend.

Cheers you our good health!

Gentle Suggestion:

Buy a juicer

Mr. Right the Juice Man

We first bought our juicer in 2007. At the time, we surmised we were not getting enough nutrients and vitamins from fruits and vegetables. After a fair amount of research, we purchased a Champion juicer, and we were off and running. Let me back up a wee bit here. A co-worker gave us a juicer a few years before we bought one. She tried it a few times and was not impressed. I happily took it home and decided to try juicing some carrots. The juice was fine, but it took twice as long to clean the juicer than it did to wash the carrots, juice, make and drink the juice! Suffice it to say we were not impressed at all, and that ended our first attempt at juicing.

We kept reading about how much a juicer would help and so fast forward to 2007 and the Champion juicer. At that time, we only juiced now and then, more as a treat than anything else. We coasted merrily along until the day we were introduced to the "c" word. That happened in 2013 and I made a promise to Daleen that I would juice for her for 5 years. Daily. No questions, no comments about it.

That was eleven and a half years ago, and I am still her personal juicer. Do not get me wrong, I drink the juice also and must admit I miss it when it is not available. Those that know me are aware I have a fondness for numbers and my juicing world is no exception. In our junk drawer is a dog tag chain that has more than four hundred steel rings, each from a 10-pound bag of carrots. Every bag we purchase has a ring (or we slip a washer on the chain when we must buy a bag with a plastic bag tie) and occasionally, I pick up the chain and show Daleen that it represents almost 430 bags or **4,300 pounds of carrots!** Really, can there be anything but goodness from that many carrots?

Our carrots get juiced together with red pepper, lemon, oranges and turmeric to make a wonderful concoction that gets the day started on a good nutritional path.

We also have a "green" juice for later in the day and it has up to fourteen different vegetables and fruits. As a much needed pick me up, I savor mine in the afternoons. Within 20 minutes of drinking the green juice, your body will be flooded with chlorophyll and you will feel the boost. I have this thing for chlorophyll and believe it to be vital.

Ogden Nash once penned these words:

> "If chlorophyll
> Cures every ill
> It would be my expectation
> That some day
> On every way
> There would be a chlorophylling station."

I can remember reading from fellow juicers that one day, I would see Daleen use a cucumber for salad or a red pepper to be grilled and I would think "Hey – I could have juiced that!" I laughed at the time, but sure enough I have had those thoughts. Juicing is interesting topic and if you announce to the world you are juicing, you will be bombarded with questions and comments. From "what do you do with the pulp" to "aren't you worried about the sugar in fruits for Daleen's cancer" and of course "What about fiber" and everything in between. **Ignore them all!** They are the people who put roadblocks in your way instead of giving you a push to help you along.

To get started you need a juicer. Duh, right? Please do not use a blender. Blenders are great for smoothies but not so much for making juice. As I mentioned, we have a Champion juicer but alas they are no longer manufactured. Personally, I believe they made them just a little too well; buy one and it will last forever. Sure, some plastic parts (external) that you use will wear out, but the machine is built like a tank! One of our cancer gurus, Chris Wark, is fond of the Noma juicer and after some research, if I had to start over, that is the kind I would buy. They are expensive, but for a lot of folks who have been diagnosed with "c," necessity trumps frugality. It is important that you juice. You can worry about what kind will last forever later, just get started. Buy the best juicer you can afford and start juicing!

The benefits of juicing are many. Chief among them is the ability to flood your system with so many good vitamins and minerals in a readily digestible and bio-available form. Another positive from juicing that is often overlooked; when you are drinking juice, you are replacing harmful choices with a healthier option. Drinking juice cuts into the time you are drinking something not as good for your body. We grow up learning that vegetables and fruit are good for you, but most people do not manage to eat enough over the course of a day. Enter juicing; it's fairly quick. It takes me about 45 minutes to an hour to make four jars of green and two "breakfast" juices. So, now that you are sold on the idea, how do you get started?

You will want to buy as many organic ingredients as you can afford. Sadly, some organics are not organic at all, and some that claim to be organic are grown with commercial fertilizer via a loophole in the methods allowed and still be called organic. Do we buy all organic? No. Juicing is not an inexpensive venture and organics are not always available or attractive in the stores. Please remember, it is far better to juice with what you have than to not juice because you cannot get all organic. If you think organics are expensive, have you priced the cost of cancer lately?

Here is a weekly shopping list for our juice:

Carrots

Red Pepper

Oranges

Lemons

Lettuce

Celery

Spinach

Apples (we prefer Granny Smith's)

Turmeric

Parsley

Kale

Cucumber

Broccoli

Pears

Swiss Chard (when available)

Watermelon

I have become quite good at knowing how much juice is in an orange just by looking at it, same for lemons. Seasonally, we grow our own kale, lettuce, Swiss Chard, spinach and parsley. I have found that a lemon and a green apple make any concoction palatable and some very tasty. However, you will need a straw as the acid from the citrus is not good for your teeth, unless you are my dentist!

Ok, let's discuss straws. Remember, glass and stainless straws are a good way to avoid adding more plastic into your body. Drink through a straw of course, as the acid in the juice is not a good thing for your dental health. For Daleen it was a matter of choice: Was drinking juice, even through a plastic straw, better than not drinking juice? Of course, the answer is a resounding yes. Glass straws can be used repeatedly (we don't want to needlessly contribute to the issue of non-biodegradable plastics in our landfills) or if you prefer, use stainless steel or paper straw. Current research is discovering some rather alarming information about most paper straws however (pfas) so please do your research. Some people will only say things that are negative about juicing, and goodness knows we do not need additional negatives in our lives. Dismiss them quickly at hand and get back to juicing! Start juicing and modify as you go along.

What is the perfect juice? It depends on your taste buds. I like both our types, but the green is my favorite. Experiment until you get the right combination for you and then do not be afraid to keep trying new things. Daleen grew Pak Choy this year and we find it tastes great in juice. Sorry for her, after juicing there was none left for cooking!

Back to ingredients. All store very well for up to a week or more and then before you use them, they must be cleaned. We use common white vinegar and water and have had no problems over the years. Some fruits do not juice well at all. Strawberries and mangoes for example, produce foam, not juice. It's hard to get much juice from Kale and if you juice broccoli, buy the broccoli with as much stem as possible.

Some experts (not sure how you become an expert on juice?) state that if you do not drink the juice right away, you will lose significant amounts of vitamins and nutrients to oxidation and decay. I am not a chemist, so I will accept their statements at face value, but even these supposed experts must admit that even a diminished number of vitamins and minerals are better than none. Store it in a Mason jar, screw the lid down tight and it stays fresh for 3-4 days.

Will you notice a change in how you feel once you start juicing? Yes. You will feel as though you have more energy and will also find that a jar of green juice makes snacking less needed or appealing. In addition to the physical component, there is the mental part. Simply put, you will know you are doing something inherently positive for your body and wellbeing; that feeling is absolutely wonderful.

You will be told that you are getting too much sugar and of course we all know that sugar feeds cancer. There is an enormous difference between sugar, that pure white poison, and natural sugars. Natural sugars are easily digestible and good for your body. When hit with those comments, ask the person "Do you juice?" The answer seems to always be "no" in our experience. That is where the conversation ends for me.

Remember I admitted a fondness for numbers? I was curious so one year, I weighed every fruit and vegetable that came into our house. We averaged 10.04 *pounds per day*. I challenge anyone now, as I have in the past, to explain how that many fruits and vegetables cannot be positive. Some of those numbers are misleading, however. A pineapple weighs quite a lot, but you must discard the top, bottom, and outer portions so you end up with far less ounces to juice than the whole pineapple. Same with lemons and oranges. Still, it is a lot of goodness.

When we travel, if it's for a couple of days, we can take juice along with us. For extended trips we rely on commercially available juice. Costly sure, but better than missing out. Check the ingredients list on any juice you purchase and watch for things you don't recognize.

A word about commercial juices. Have you ever juiced an orange or a lemon? The product is different with each piece of fruit you juice. But when you go to the grocery store and look at the juice aisle, the juices are uniform in color! How is that possible? The answer is that the juices are blended, filtered, treated in some cases so that the product is uniformly pleasing to the eye. Some even have food coloring for uniformity. Apparently in these great United States, we won't drink (or eat) something unless it looks like Madison Avenue has portrayed it to be! Unfortunately, that also means that the mass-produced commercial juice really isn't a good source of goodness. Some nutritional experts have called commercially available juice "dead", meaning the only benefit is from the fact it's a liquid. Avoid them if you are thinking about a cancer protocol. Real juice doesn't need to be fortified with anything; the goodness is there.

Now let's talk about money, the least favorite subject for many. Juicing is not inexpensive, but you are not juicing to save money. Rather you are juicing to stay healthy and vibrant. Perspective is everything and it applies to juicing. Do we shop for deals? Of course. We try to be fiscally responsible people. There are only so many corners to cut when purchasing (or growing) vegetables and fruits, however. In the summertime, items such as lettuce and watermelon are inexpensive and plentiful. Not so much in the winter and spring months. Remember the reason why you are juicing and grin and bear it. Oranges are much less expensive in the winter, apples in the fall so eventually it evens out. I honestly believe there is no better, or less expensive, way to get as many nutrients into your body as you can by juicing. If you must cut corners elsewhere, do it! You'll reap the rewards with better health.

Now, onto time. Making 4 or 5 jars of green juice and two jars of morning juice with our juicer takes me about an hour. Think about that. An hour a day, 6 days a week, 52 weeks in a year. In the past 11 years, that equates to 312 hours or almost two full weeks. Spent juicing! There is no better way for me to demonstrate to Daleen that it's important to me that she has jars of goodness every day. Remember that fun word perspective? From my perspective, that is time well spent. It's a labor of love, commitment, and dedication. The newer juicers might take less time, but remember, time is a commodity we all share. The only determining factor is how we choose to spend it. When you juice, you are choosing to spend some of your time on health and goodness.

Gentle Suggestion

Buy the best juicer you can afford and start juicing now.
Any fresh juice is better than no juice!

Clean Your Junk Drawer

Everyone has a dirty little secret. It looks normal, and innocent on the outside; the inside is a whole other story, every household has one, the *Junk* drawer. (There is no shame, remember? I offer no judgment.) Oh, you KNOW I am going to connect this to our good health!

I am talking about that one kitchen drawer that sort of sticks and only opens a third of the way. There seems to be a piece of card stock folded causing the drawer to jam open, just far enough to bravely stick your fingers in. For the drawer to open completely, you have to put your hand in with fingers splayed flat and wiggle the offending coupon down. Mystery solved, it was a Bed Bath and Beyond coupon for 20% off. Even if the coupon had not expired in 2021, as of 2023 the store unfortunately is permanently closed.

Oh look, there is a flat button clock battery. Not sure which clock it fits, nor do I know if it works. Hey, there is a package of shoe laces. There is one, short handled screw driver with paint on it, two keys to a home we no longer live in, a harmonica with a bit of rust, a 1 inch plastic naked baby doll, and a yellow sticky (no longer sticky) note with an unknown phone number, written in red ink. There is one, in good condition combination lock that is closed. We have absolutely no idea the correct numbers. We randomly try different birthdates, anniversaries, lucky numbers, and so forth. Why do we torture ourselves?

Then there are the pens. Two adults live in this house, why do we need 62 pens? In the olden days of phone calls with an actual curly cord, while gabbing and doodling I would sit near the junk drawer and "test" pens to see if they still worked. It felt useful to toss all pens that were dried up. Apparently, I stopped doing that free service 19 years ago. We have an impressive collection of old, non-usable pens. Also slipped in the side of the drawer is a wooden ruler. On the back it has a list of US Presidents and the words "United States Rulers", the last one on the list was from 2009.

It is time to take Marie Kondo words to heart, "If it doesn't spark joy, toss it out."

The cabinetry looks good on the surface, however inside is a nightmare.

When vacuuming up the debris and crumbs, you ask, are those food crumbs? How did those end up in the junk drawer? Each item we put back (for at least a month or so) is critically analyzed. Is it clean, needed, in working order, all good questions.

It was far past time for a fresh start.

> **"If you don't take care of this the most magnificent machine that you will ever be given...where are you going to live?"**
>
> KARYN CALABR

"Detoxification aids in strengthening the immune system rejuvenate skin and boost mental health. Detoxifying brings balance back to your life and helps your system function correctly." www.evolutwellness.com

While your body may look normal and innocent on the outside... your insides could most likely be a sluggish, toxic, chemical laden, jumbled mess.

Common sense reminds us to keep our machine in good working condition. On a daily basis we come in contact with many pollutants: air we breathe, food we eat, drinking water, chemicals, toxins, fungus, parasites and metals. The simple action of cleaning out some of the junk appears to be a wise move. David "Avocado" Wolfe, Dr. Bryan Ardis, and Dr. Lee Merritt, each brilliant minds willing to share the advantages and protocols of cleaning out parasites and toxins.

The order of the day is perhaps a serious detox on a quarterly basis, weekly or even daily choices to keep our machine well oiled and working smoothly and in tip top shape. I will share several ideas as a starting place for you to research and bravely dig a little deeper.

> **"Life depends on change and renewal."**
>
> PATRICK TROUGHTON

In the form of ideas and suggestions to remove toxic waste, parasites, radiation, pollution and damaged cells in our bodies, I offer you **Practical Hope**.

Asparagus - contains glutathione which is great for fighting off infectious cells

Broccoli – boosts the liver's ability to regulate chemical levels in the body

Artichokes – two phytonutrients to help produce bile which aids in digestion and removing harmful toxins

Beets – contains betaine and pectin, both of which clear toxins in the body

Strawberries – the fibrous outer seeds help draw out toxins

Lemons – boost liver function which helps enhance the body's detox functions

Basil - contains phenolic and antioxidant compounds both have internal house-keeping duties

Cilantro – absorbs heavy metals, a wise choice after an x-ray or flight

Parsley – clears toxins and heavy metals, another good choice after an x-ray or flight

Rosemary – promotes the flow of bile to help remove toxins

Seeds – Pumpkin, Sunflower, Watermelon, Flax, and Sesame Seeds each offer insoluble and soluble fiber to help eliminate toxins. Chia seeds are amazingly helpful as they absorb 30 times their weight in moisture making them an excellent choice for helping to remove toxic waste from the body

> "He who has health has hope; and he
> who has hope has everything."
>
> ARABIC PROVERB

Baking Soda and salt baths – after any radiation exposure

Bentinite Clay – named for Fort Benton, Wyoming. Removes pesticides, lead and heavy metals

Apple Pectin – it helps purge toxins from the bloodstream through bile

Activated Charcoal – absorbs bacteria in the intestines, it binds with by-products

Rebounding – stimulates a free flowing lymphatic system that will efficiently drain away the toxins.

Dry Brushing – activates the lymphatic system

Selenium – use after receiving contrast dye called Gadolinium during MRI

EDTA – powerful detox of toxic heavy metals: Lead, Aluminum and Mercury

Fasting and Cleansing – both powerful ways to clean out the junk and refresh

Chlorella - It is effective in removing heavy metals and other harmful compounds from the body

Gentle Suggestion

Clean your junk drawer.

Put on your Armor

> Every single cancer patient has a
> compromised immune system.

Woah, Nellie, that sentence seems harsh. It's best to get over that feeling, push up your sleeves, and get to work. *By the way*, that same statement can very well be said of common sicknesses, like the flu bug as well as heart disease, diabetes, dementia, shingles, Crohn's, Alzheimer's and other serious illness and diseases of today.

The Mayo Clinic shares a study that is slightly alarming. As of 2022, only 2.7%of the American population has been deemed healthy. That means we are aggressively hurting ourselves.

We have co-existed with external pathogens for thousands of years. Our bodies have an innate intelligence that is constantly working to keep us alive.

We need to take responsibility for our own health and a mighty immune system is our first line of defense.

Rather than being a "nutty know it all" about our environment and work to dominate nature or fight a war against germs, we absolutely need to work in harmony with nature.

The Terrain Theory of Antoine Bechamp puts the emphasis on maintaining a state of wellness and internal balance to stave off disease.

In my mind, I liken this to the armor of God. The armor of God represents the defense we must take in our spiritual lives. The armor of Health and Wellness is our immune system. It needs to be strong so that you can stand firm against illness and disease (dis-ease).

The Germ Theory popularized by Louis Pasteur, focuses on external pathogens (bacteria and viruses) invading our body.

I think of this as the run and hide theory. Stay away from crowds with germs, wear gloves to avoid germs, wearing a paper mask to keep germs at bay and so forth. **Most people come in contact with 60,000 germs on a daily basis.**

If I am going to spout off being a card-carrying member of the (1850) Antoine Bechamp fan club, I had better list some things that help keep my immune system vital, vibrant and robust.

The immune system is a set of cells whose function is to protect the body against unknown substances or microorganisms.

Over the course of a couple months, through all my page turning, highlighting, and note taking, I continued to stumble upon this idea: if you don't want to get sick or want to heal from sickness, then build your immune system. If this is indeed true with stacks of facts to back it up ...and I have found nothing to the contrary, then it should be/was/is my mission to heal my immune system.

The goal should be to build an intense, strong, armor proof, immune system.

How do you do that?

I will list some of the things I learned. I gave every single one of them my attention and the old college try. Please note: while these things are not magical and 100% bullet proof, I can truthfully say that I have experienced the sniffles for 2 days, ONCE in the last decade.

My immune system is running in one direction, **full steam ahead!**

Buckle up Buttercup! Some ideas cost money, some are hard to do, some take time. More than likely you will at one time or another become frustrated, swear or even cry. Surprisingly, there are even ideas that are free. Even before the list starts, here is your first one, and boy howdy is it a gem. While you continue to read, take this book outside and read these words in the sunshine, both easy and free.

Before you begin reading and highlighting the list, let me give you the long and short of it. Bad news first, sadly, there is not a magic pill that will fix everything. Good News, YES, you can heal, rebuild and thrive with a fabulous, strong, running full tilt, immune system.

By no means is this a complete list. I encourage you to take that purple pen on your night stand and write on this page. Fill in the margins, write down what you learned, things I missed and or forgot to add to this list.

Here are some things that I use to build up, strengthen and keep my immune system in tip top shape. They have contributed to my strong immunity.

On the flip side of the healthy coin, if you do nothing and expect to stay well for the long run and not miss a day of work or school…I think you can guess what is going to happen.

One note before we begin going through a list of ideas and **Practical Hope**. As you may already be aware, good to mention once again, antibiotics, in serious cases, can most certainly be lifesaving. That being said, if you do take antibiotics, it will compromise your gut health dramatically. Typically it will take time, 6 months or more to balance the micro biome to healthy diverse bacteria levels. We all know that a healthy gut micro biome translates into a vital immune system that creates a healthy thriving person.

Sunshine

The sun's UV rays help your body make the nutrient, Vitamin D. This hormone is synthesized through the skin and it is critical for a healthy immune system. With constant exposure to sunlight, you can help strengthen it. As little as 15 minutes daily will do the trick. Getting just 3 minutes of sunshine, within 15 minutes of awakening helps with sleep at night…better sleep equates to better immune system. Sunshine helps us maintain calcium to prevent brittle bones. It also reduces stress. An added benefit of being in the sunshine, it boosts your level of serotonin. That is the chemical that improves your mood and helps you stay calm.

If you live in a gray, cloudy, at times limited sunny northern area….you may want to look into eating oodles of cooked mushrooms. Amazingly mushrooms grow in mainly gray and rainy areas, this is most certainly is a glimpse of a beautiful harmonious creation. People in these areas, can also benefit from full spectrum lighting.

Beta Glucan
Beta Glucan acts as an immunomodulating agent (helps fight disease) through the activation of innate immune cells.

If I could only afford one supplement, this would be my top choice.

www.ancientelements.com They have a video that explains how Beta Glucan works in our bodies.

Break up with your Microwave
Even short term use is known to weaken your immune system. The heat found in a microwave changes the molecular structure of your food, changing the nutrient value. The radiation in a microwave produces cancer-causing agents and leads to abnormal changes in human blood, weakening the immune system. More research on your part might be in order.

Fluoride
Chronic exposure to fluoride at 1ppm could have a long-term detrimental effect on the general health of the population. www.fluoridealert.org

> "In point of fact, fluoride causes more human cancer death, and causes it faster than any other chemical."
>
> DR. DEAN BURK, PH.D.

Yes, fluoride has a detrimental and sometimes deadly effect on your immune system.

Bee Pollen
One bee needs to work eight hours a day for one month to gather one teaspoon of bee pollen. Bee Pollen is a food source and protein for bees. However, we can benefit from it as well. Bee Pollen blocks and reduces inflammation, boost energy, fights allergies, has prebiotic properties, and can lower cholesterol to name a few wonderful benefits. Bee pollen has been found to increase the immune system

response against infection and disease. Amazingly, bee pollen extract was found to kill potentially harmful bacteria.

Sleep

Sleep is one of the best defense mechanisms for immunity. Not enough consistent good quality sleep and you & your immune system will pay the price.

A great night's sleep plays a crucial role in our immune system being robust. In fact, sleep contributes to both innate and adaptive immunity. In your bedroom, remove all EMF's (electromagnetic fields). EMFs emit radiation. Common sources of EMFs are televisions, cell phones, baby monitors, laptops etc. You know how dark it is in a quality hotel room? Make your bedroom as dark. Use a sleep mask if you can't afford light darkening curtains. According to those in the know, ideal temperature for a better night's sleep is 68-69 degrees. Be consistent with bedtime and wake up time. Whenever possible get 3 minutes of direct sunshine upon waking up.

Eat Fermented foods

80% of your immune system is in your gut.

(Before I continue, may I say, I dislike using the word "gut". However, I loathe typing the words, gastrointestinal (GI) system, so going forth, I will grudgingly use the word, gut.) Grab a spoonful of Sauerkraut, Miso, and Kimchee, cultured vegetables, drink some Kefir or Kombucha, while listening to a Donna Schwenk podcast or while reading her book, Cultured Foods for Life.

Stop All Artificial Dyes

Our immune system finds it difficult to defend the body against artificial dyes. Food dyes harm your gut, promote inflammation, and are immune disrupting and some are carcinogenic. Just seems like bad Mojo all around.

Note: If you are going to purchase store bought cookies – you might consider buying some produced internationally. Many other countries have very strict laws regarding not using or limited use of artificial dyes.

Stop Alcohol
Drinking weakens your immune system. Alcohol reduces the number of bacteria your system needs. It also reduces the number of antibodies available to fight off infection.

6 drinks a week, 40% higher rate for getting breast cancer

10 drinks a week, 70% higher rate for getting breast cancer

Enough said.

Detox your liver
A healthy, well functioning liver is needed for a healthy immunity. Hello, dark leafy greens of goodness; spinach, kale, arugula, mustard greens, bitter gourd and chicory contain cleansing compounds that help in detoxifying the liver. Oh, and more good choices, blueberries and cranberries clean the liver naturally as well.

Elderberry
The berries and flowers of elderberry are packed with antioxidants and vitamins that can boost your immune system.

Eat healthy fats
Eating healthy fats help keep inflammation in check and regulate immune cell activity. Seeds, nuts, avocados, coconut oil, wild caught Pacific salmon, dark chocolate to name a few.

Oxygen

> **The cause of cancer is no longer a mystery; we know it occurs whenever any cell is denied 60% of its oxygen requirements.**

Oxygen translates into more cellular energy, thus increasing immune strength. A couple ideas to look into and do a little research on are: a hyperbaric chamber, 35% food grade hydrogen peroxide, sparkling water, hydrogen water and sodium bicarbonate.

Grounding/Earthing

Earthing neutralizes free radicals, and as a result, the immune response calms down – contributing to a faster rate of healing.

> "Earthing the most important health discovery ever."
>
> CLINTON OBER

Infared Bio-mat

Increases your body core temperature and directly tunes up the immune system by creating fever conditions. Research shows cancer cells dying (apoptosis) after 4 months of use. There are several different sizes as well as price points available, we chose the Richway biomat 7000. We have used it for nine years and are very pleased with results and our purchase.

www.thebiomatshop.com

Red Light Therapy

Red light therapy strengthens your immune system. Red light therapy delivers therapeutic wavelengths of natural light to your skin and cells.

www.mitoredlight.com

Chaga

Called a mushroom, it's actually a parasite that grows on the Birch Tree. ***This is the MOST immune nourishing substance on earth.*** It is actually intelligent in the way it adapts to the immune system.

www.birchboys.com

Stop using Anti-bacterial soaps and cleaners

Anti-bacterial soaps and cleaners kill good bacteria, too.

Air Filter

Open your home windows (no matter the temperature) for at least 20 minutes each day. Clean out that air. While you are at it, how about changing your home furnace filter every 60 days. Seriously consider saving up and buying and indoor air filter. If you body does not have to work hard to clean the air you breathe, it can spend more time on helping you heal and thrive. We are very happy with our Air Doctor. Remember, if you don't have an air filter, YOU are the filter.

www.airdoctorpro.com

Rethink needless pharmaceuticals and over the counter drugs

No one is deficient in any pharmaceutical drugs. Your immune system has to work at recognizing a foreign substance. I choose to have my immune system work at building my immunity not fussing over scrubbing clean foreign substances.

Practice something that you love: Believe it or not, watercolor painting, cross stitching, quilting, playing chess, beading, crocheting, martial arts, dancing, baking etc....all build your immune system

Tapping (meditation for others) for me, this has reduced my anxiety, stress and fretting. Less stress is a very good thing when it comes to a well functioning immune system. The Tapping Solution by Nick Ortner

Watch a funny movie

Laugher improves blood vessel function; so needless to say, laughter boosts your immune system.

Cold exposure

Evidence suggests that cold water therapy can stimulate our body's immune system.

Exercise

Moderate exercise mobilizes immune system cells, helping the body defend itself against pathogens. Rebounding, bike riding, swimming, walking on the beach, cleaning out the chicken coop, gardening, rebounding, walk your dog, all movement helps build our immune systems.... get moving, friends. Here is a great fact, Patrick Quillin shares, "A half hour of exercise every other day cuts the risk for breast cancer by 75%".

Iodine

Deficiency in iodine can greatly diminish the strength of our immune system. I came across two books which both helped me learn and understand the healing nature of Iodine.

Dr. David Brownstein wrote an informative and educational book called, Iodine why you need it and why you can't live without it. Dr. Mark Sircus wrote an exceptional book entitled, Healing with Iodine Your Missing Link to Better Health.

Both books are worthy of your time.

Food

Eat Clean Non-toxic Food

garlic, ginger, lemon, spinach, broccoli, sweet potatoes, blueberries, oily fish, salmon, nuts, oranges, raw honey, acerola cherries, guava, citrus fruits, mushrooms, liver, fish oil, dark green leafy vegetables, capers, bell peppers, onions, apples, almonds, turmeric

Supplements (bio-available only, made from food source)

Selenium: the immune system needs Selenium to work properly. It also boosts white blood cells.

Quercetin: an antioxidant, eliminates free radicals

Vitamin A: in its preformed form (retinol) in animal sources, and in its precursor form carotenoid present in vegetables

Vitamin C: antioxidant nutrient

Copper: this mineral is essential for good absorption of vitamin c. Copper increases the production of white blood cells (which make up the immune system).

Intermittent fasting

Helps strengthen your immune system. Fasting also stimulates the white blood cells. 80% of your immune system is in your gut.

A few preliminary human trials have shown a decrease in risk for cancer or a decrease in cancer growth rates. Cancer cells have 10-70 times more insulin receptor cells.

Fasting helps lower insulin and correct insulin resistance (Dr. Eric Berg, DC)

Seek Positive Write down 3 things that are positive about you!
1.

2.

3.

Go ahead write in this book! You bought it, use it, highlight, doodle, use stickers, dog ear the pages and for goodness sakes underline the good parts. It's okay, there are no book police.

Natural (non-synthetic) Essential Oils Dipping your toes into the fascinating world of essential oils will positively help with healing. While there are many reputable companies, I like to purchase from www.zenithsuppies.com and www.mountainroseherbs.com I have been very pleased with all of my purchases.

Before I list some most helpful oils, I would like to slip in the explanation of anti-microbial. It is a substance that kills micro-organisms such as bacteria or mold, or stops them from growing and causing disease.

Lavender: Anti-viral, anti-microbial, anti-bacteria, relieves stress, boosts markers of immune function, promotes immune system health

Lemon: Powerful toxin fighting properties helps the immune system

Peppermint: Contains menthol which is anti-viral, anti-bacterial and has anti-inflammatory properties, thus the perfect choice to boost the immune system

Tea Tree: Melaleuca, one of the most effective and useful oils for immune system support. Outstanding anti-microbial properties and its ability to stimulate the immune system which helps fight off infection and disease.

Eucalyptus: Builds immunity to avoid coughs, cold and flu

Cinnamon: Warming effect, anti-microbial, anti-septic properties, immune boosting

Black Pepper: Woody spicy oil that strengthens the immune system

Cloves: Restorative and stimulating effects on the immune system

Sandalwood: Woody, sweet aroma, affinity with the respiratory system and anti-septic, so is healing for immunity

Gentle Suggestion

This might be a good time to read the
Antoine Bechamp vs. Louis Pasteur theories.

Pink, Pink you Stink

I chose the path less traveled, and I did not "join" the pink club. Instead of joining in by wearing pink boas and pink tutus, I went a different direction that was a better fit for me.

Every single week, Mr. Right brings me flowers. About 10 years ago, he considerately stopped bringing me my favorite pink posies.

I adored all shades of the color pink and it was my favorite. However, I can vividly remember the "closet day". I went to my closet and started ripping down anything that was pink. There were pink t-shirts, pink fleece jacket, pink oxford shirt, pale pink tank top, pink glittery tank, and a long pink granny gown.

Next I stepped over to my dresser. I tossed into the pile a pink slip, a pale pink lovely piece of lingerie and some new pink undies. I threw them in the trash can for pick up the next day. Done, moving on, I brushed my hands of that. Flipping through clothing catalogs; I was drawn to the pink, but chose black, gray or taupe.

Imagine being so broken that for a time, I couldn't even read, bake, write, cook or sew? All without the happy color pink to cheer me up.

Then I would catch sight of a pink bucket of Kentucky Fried Chicken, pink Jell-O, pink diet soda, pink gummy vitamins, pink garbage bags, pink cake mix, professional football players wearing pink cleats or socks, the referees using pink whistles, pink menu card in the airline seat pocket and on and on the ridiculous nonsense went. Not one of those things would help me heal. The chemicals, sugar and colorings would only add gasoline to the fire, and the stupidity of pink garbage bags or pink furnace filters was and is an assault on my intelligence.

The cancer death rate has only improved 5% since 1950. While we have had several presidents declare "war" on cancer, the rate of cancer cases continues to rise. According to the National Cancer Institute as of 2022, each day 1,600 Americans die from cancer. www.cancer.gov

We all know that drug companies make billions in profit every year. If for a moment you can set aside your personal feelings, the drug companies are a business and they have shareholders to answer to. Their job is to increase the bottom line. Their job is not to cure patients; their job is to make money. Yes, that is a hard pill to swallow.

Chemotherapy and radiotherapy are both intrinsically carcinogenic treatments.

> ## "There are more people making a living from cancer than people who are dying from cancer."
>
> DARIN OLIEN

October rolls around and we are all SMACKED in the face with Pinktober. It is a yearly propaganda force that is helping spread the word about breast cancer awareness. Who among us has not heard of breast cancer? Why do we need to be reminded?

Every print ad, radio and television commercial, team uniforms, car lot flying pink balloons, specialty candle, pajamas set, cupcakes, boxed cake mix, soup can, printed bank check, rubber bracelets, shower gel , stuffed animals, fleece vest, button, tumblers, and hair ties all are PINK and all are for the cure. How exactly is a printed check going to help someone who has been diagnosed with breast cancer? Will it help her remember she has cancer?

News Flash! I can absolutely, with 100% certainty tell you, once you have been diagnosed, you will NEVER live another day without remembering.

Our family is not buying into it. Several years ago, we changed Pinktober to **SOCKTOBER!** Our family, cleans out our sock drawers, we toss old, worn out socks. We purchase new and while we are at the store, all our charity money for the month goes towards... you guessed it, buying and donating socks to those in need!!!!! The number one request on homeless shelters wish lists are ...SOCKS! This is a project we can whole heartedly support. Nothing mysterious here, buy the socks, donate the socks, people wear the socks, it is all very clear cut.

How does donating money in the name of "let's cure cancer" to a walk-a-thons, or bake sales flush out? How does walking for 3 days to make money for a company when 79% of the money raised goes towards salaries and administration costs, be anything but sad and unethical? Increasing their bottom line because of someone else's misfortune seems shameful.

How does donating coins to a jar in a store help breast cancer patients' work? I was a breast cancer patient; no one gave me a jar with coins to buy a tube of organic lipstick or a shopping cart of organic vegetables. Fortunately I do not need a donation jar. I am curious and wonder where and who are these patients that received the donations?

Before donating, I urge you to do your due diligence. You might consider reading the book, <u>Pink Ribbon Blues</u> by Gayle A. Sulik . Or you could take some time and watch a documentary called *Pink Ribbons*, Inc. by filmmaker Lea Pool.

Or here is a brilliant practical idea: If you have a friend or family member or are made aware of someone diagnosed with breast cancer or ANY cancer for that matter, maybe consider donating directly to them. Give a grocery card to purchase organic carrots for juicing. Consider contributing to their wish list: help them buy new sneakers, a Rebound-Air or a juicer etc.

Right in the middle of a beautiful, lovely week, an awesome-sauce date night at the Space Needle was about to happen and quietly without fanfare, I took a giant step toward healing. After 7 years of angst, I needed to bravely make a change.

I chose to wear a brand new, very cute black and white pencil skirt along with an adorable smoky gray, encrusted with jewels, sweater tied casually around my shoulders, and a color saturated pink blouse. I paired it all with a stunning pair of my grandmother's antique pink earrings.

Once I was done thinking it over for the 1,000th time, I decided to wear it. It might not have seemed like a huge deal to most, to me it was monumental. As always, Mr. Right complimented me several times. Not one person pointed or even noticed the pink. No other human being in the restaurant even gave the color a second thought. It was a humongous step for me towards healing and no one seemed to care.

I got to thinking about the view, the food, the piano music, my manicure, the card he gave me, how tight my Spanks were (I was just seeing if you were paying attention), how I loved taste testing his food and sharing mine, how cute and remarkably comfortable my peep toe shoes were, my pedicure, how much I enjoyed the after dinner coffee, the bracelet I wore, how much I enjoyed the conversation, how much I enjoy spying Mr. Right politely and smoothly tipping the young valet, how nice the car drive home was and yeah, I sort of forgot to fuss and fret over wearing pink. For the first time in ages, the color didn't seem to matter.

That night was the beginning of my heart starting to heal. I started making my way back to liking the color pink again.

> "Sometimes the smallest step in the right
> direction ends up being the biggest step of your
> life. Tip toe if you must, but take the step."
>
> NAEEM CALLAWAY

Maybe after years of healing, Pink, pink you are just sort of smelly.

To me, that smells like progress.

Gentle Suggestion

While looking through pink colored glasses, try not to allow yourself to be bamboozled and bullied into donating to causes you have not investigated. Take your time and think it through. Being a good steward with your charitable funds is an admirable and noble trait.

"Friends"

One of the questions I often get asked is, "Did you lose any friends?"

"The shifts of fortune test the reliability of friends."

CICERO

I will tell you the truth.

Buckle up, it's not pretty.

People were/are scared of my cancer label. They don't want to catch what I have. I don't blame them. I don't wish this on any soul.

I cried and still cry about the friends I have lost. I can almost hear you saying out loud, they were not your real friends to begin with. Okay, I hear you and agree with you loud and clear. Sure in fourth grade you learn that friends change and move on. However, when the going gets tough and you are in your 50's and friends start jumping ship it is quite a shock and your heart breaks. Your feelings get hurt. Your spirit is smashed. No matter your age, it is difficult to make a whole new group of friends. Very quickly, the days become extremely lonely.

Ten plus years later, I was listening to Laura Story and her song, "Blessings". Isn't it funny how and when we need to learn huge lessons, those lessons arrive in sometimes unique ways? In her lyrics, you come across the insightful and poignant thought…"What if your healing comes through tears? What if the trials of your life are Your (God's) mercies in disguise?"

The invitations to lunch, dinner, coffee, slowly slipped away. I don't think most wanted to be mean, I think they were scared of my diagnosis and really didn't know what to say or do.

"Yet God will use them to help develop you and to direct you, for you will see that you must go where you are celebrated and not just tolerated"

DR. JOHN STANKO

We stopped getting invited to activities. Folks stopped sending messages.

It was just such a powerful stunning slap in the face, a rude wakeup call. For some silly reason, I thought my friends would circle the wagons, and support me.

I was gob smacked that I was duped into what I thought were sincere friendships. It was the shocking realization of what a poor judge of character I really was.

This lesson in friends shattered my confidence in my ability to read people and of course makes me wonder how many more "friends" might be hiding in plain sight.

News flash, when the doodoo hit the fan, Mr. Right stood by my side ...and that was enough.

While the owners of his company were kind and compassionate people, at some point in this journey, he went back to work, talked with other humans, married people, went to work lunches and had to travel for business.

Even today, as I write this, my stomach feels weird and I get a lump in my throat about how many of my personal friendships vanished. The silence is palpable.

There are a couple of beautiful exceptions. I remember them with **exquisite crystal clarity.**

My sister-in-law, Janis was the one and ONLY person who while living on the other side of the country would let me phone her daily and cry. She listened to me cuss like I have never cussed before. Then miraculously, she would pick up the phone the next day. She was one of the people that guided me back to health. She was instrumental in helping me heal. She is an angel among us.

A young neighbor, 30 years younger than me, who would car pool with Mr. Right now and then, stopped by one evening. She brought the ugliest bouquet of dyed flowers I ever did see. They were beautiful to me. She also made a pan of the driest brownies made with coconut flour I have ever sampled. She said I know you are probably trying to eat healthy so I baked these for you. Her kindness and generous spirit took my breath away. She lifted me up and helped me heal.

One family friend was over the top generous with her time and kindness. Unfortunately, she knew the drill. She already had gone down the cancer path. She called me and let me vent and ask questions and cry and ask more questions. Here is the remarkable thing about her...she and I chose to heal very differently. She NEVER ONCE judged me. She lifted me up without question. With grace & a kind heart she gave me hope. She helped me heal.

Our niece attending college on the other side of the country sent a box of goodness. A box stuffed full of dollar store things to make me smile. A BIG fat "diamond" ring, socks, note pads, pens, a crown and on and on the list of goodies went. She wrote a thoughtful card. College kids are not known for having extra money or time or the inclination to go to the post office. It made me feel a whole lot better. She lifted me up and helped me heal.

Of course, our adult children were supportive. They sent cards, flowers, offered telephone calls and jokes on a daily basis. They made me laugh. From one son & daughter in law, I received flower bulbs and that gave me my first **hope**! They gave me thinking about the future back. The flower bulbs "told" me, I would be around to see them grow and bloom. Another daughter in law filled our freezer with healthy vegan soup. It was easy to take one out the night before and thaw for lunch the next day. One son took me target shooting. Boy howdy, was that a stress reliever. I felt powerful and in charge of something. I brought home my practice target. It was a spirit lifter for sure. The four of them lifted me up and helped me heal.

I did receive and saved several cards to re-read for a positive lift. Some cards made my day; other cards pushed me over the edge and made me sob. Some would include a kind hand written note.

Note to reader: If you ever need to send a card to a person trying to heal from cancer, please don't choose a card that says cancer. The person is well aware of the hot water they are drowning in.

Some folks sent a card and I never heard from them again. That was their way of dealing with my situation. They signed their name and washed their hands of me. They sent a card and now their "obligation" was fulfilled.

Here is a sampling of comments or actions that hurt my feelings and I am typing them, in hopes of relinquishing them from my memory.

Pink cocoa "I know you don't like pink and can't have sugar, but this had the pink ribbon on it and I just knew you would like it".

One childhood friend came over and brought 4 Starbucks coffees and donuts then had to leave quickly. I did not hear from her again for 3 years.

Two years after diagnosis, while browsing in a fabric store…"Daleen! You're still alive! I thought you would have died by now."

A miniature pink rose bush "I know you don't like pink, but this reminded me of you and you will look back and be glad you got this disease, you will be stronger for it."

18 months after my diagnosis, a cheerful bouquet of flowers was delivered to me. "I just didn't know if you would make it."

Asked to Bruce, "Which breast had cancer and what stage is she, so I can pray for her".

A friend of 34 years came to town on vacation. I worked up the courage to be truthful and say I didn't feel up to having dinner out. I have not heard from her since.

"We are just waiting for the other shoe to drop."

One day, while ironing, I was on the telephone with a "good friend" of many years. I worked up the courage to tell her my diagnosis. Yes, it does take courage to tell folks what you are going through. I was shocked & gob smacked, that phone call was the last I ever heard from her.

I received a Prayer book. The "friend" suggested that I needed to pray more for if I had this would not have happened.

A 30+ year friendship, sort of continued to bump along only if I didn't bring up me being sick. We just talked about her and the weather. To offer her grace, I will say, I guess she didn't know what to do or say to me. It was okay for a while. I felt like I was measuring my words as not to offend her with how I was actually doing.

One "friend" just didn't mention me being sick. Didn't ask how I was. Just pretended it didn't exist and it would all just go away. If I did slip and mention I wasn't feeling tip top that day, she would say, "awwww".

Most friends, just sort of quietly stopped checking in.

One "friend" sent pages of Bible verses. She said the reason I "came down" with cancer is I wasn't reading the Bible enough.

A person sent a pink China dish and a pink ribbon pin. "I know you collect these dishes and don't care for the pink but I just knew you will like this one."

"You healing naturally from cancer was just a fluke."

Another person, strongly suggested I just have a decent meal of a good steak, a glass of milk, potatoes and a small dessert.

Words can and do smash your spirit.

> "This is how we know we are healing, when we
> stop letting "their" words (those who have hurt us)
> be "the" words over our lives, and we start letting
> "God's Word" be the final word in our lives."
>
> WORD ALIVE CONFERENCE

When someone did ask how I was doing, I tried telling somewhat of the truth. Quickly, they just got off the phone or ended the conversation.

I was so starved for a friend to talk to, I learned to lie.

Obviously my brain wasn't working at top speed. I somehow twisted my thinking into going easy on my "friends" so they would feel okay; in the process I continued to crush my high standards, values and my very soul.

I said I was fine and dandy. That let them off the hook. No, it did not help me, not in the least. It just extended the days and months that I would dissolve into tears.

Hopefully, writing this book, will allow my truth telling to begin and continue towards healing.

Here is the good news portion of this chapter... my husband suggested I put on his old Army boots and STOMP the HELL out of that pink rose bush.

He also wrapped the piece of pink china in paper and with a hammer, let me crush it to powder.

He actually told the person that he threw the pin away. She was stunned. It was specifically not asked for and they did it anyway.

It was amazing how awkward it felt to hear, yet, how empowering I felt at the same time. Mr. Right heard me! I wasn't invisible and he wasn't going to be polite about it, in any fashion.

To say, I had to learn to set boundaries was the understatement of the year.

Also, I had to learn to not be so polite, certainly a huge lesson for me to explore, unravel to and implement. Marcus Ellis brings up a huge (to me) subject called being caught up in the "nice" process. Being nice to bullies, disrespectful medical personal as well as so called friends have not done me any favors. I am learning to not be a doormat. It is a big change for me, yet by golly I am working on being a bit more vocal and in a kind and direct way standing up for myself.

After several years, I have begun to search for "my tribe". I continue to look for folks who think about healing and wellness somewhat like I do. Come to find out, those amazing people are hard to find. That's maybe one reason, you may have purchased this book. I, too look forward with hope to making new friends.

I have yet to find someone who chose the same pathway as me. One day, I will be brave enough to go to a conference and meet like minded folks. One day, I will stand and be honest about my health choices and feel proud about me. One day in the future, I will not be bullied.

Being treated poorly and spoken to in a rather distasteful, ill mannered, unkind, despicable, harsh, mean way IS being a bullied. I have chosen to no longer be a doormat. Most likely, I will not scream back, that is just not my personality. I have garnered enough courage to at least say, I am done. You are not being nice.

Saying no to bullies is hard. Each day I am becoming stronger and more vocal.

> **"Sometimes you've got to put on your big girl boots and prove that you can use the pointy end."**
>
> CURLY GIRL DESIGNS

This book is the beginning of me being honest.

I needed/wanted to make new friends. I reached out to a hobby community on social media. Yes, I have met a few people in person. A couple of people have become good friends. It is a pleasure to talk about a hobby we have in common. For now, that feeds my soul and helps me through the tricky days of continued healing.

There are a handful of honest to goodness, sincere friends. Those folks will lift you up and stand in your corner for the long run. Our elders would say, if you can count on one hand the number of friends you have, then you are truly blessed.

You can count me, through these pages, as someone you describe as a sincere friend. I wish for you goodness, health and a vibrant, interesting life.

I won't slip away. I stick. You can count on me to stand silently in your corner and not judge you. I will offer you practical hope and help you find it. This is me, CHEERING you on! If I run into you in a fabric store or a book store, I will hug you and celebrate with you!!!

Gentle Suggestion

"Stay close to people who feel like sunlight."

XAN OHU

Grace and Free Will

Our 30 plus year friendship included so many good things: our birthdays were a day apart, we thought it was funny to go out to lunch and buy each other's meal, we shared the same middle names. We met and quickly became tied together as forever friends when we were young Rainbow girls (Masonic Order). Our love of dogs, flowers, the color red, popcorn, organization, hobbies and sparkly things kept us in each other's back pockets.

We shared our love of sewing and counted cross-stitch. The day after a big famous wedding or fashion show, it was always fun to talk about the dresses.

My childhood friend chose a different medical path. She passed away from cancer 4 years after I was diagnosed. The doctors gave her 18 months to live, she fulfilled their prophecy.

One of the things about healing naturally is that it is a personal choice. One of the great things about being my age is that you know better than to force your ideas on others. I most certainly do not want people to tell me what I should do.

Holding hands with a friend who chose an opposite path to healing is one of the toughest things I have had to do. My good friend as well as other friends and family have selected very different pathways. Of course, I send cards, bring flowers and food, share a joke, and fill their refrigerator with soup; we just don't share healing strategies.

It is tricky, hard and it hurts. You are awash with sadness aware that you are losing your friend. However, your friend has 100% faith in allopathic doctors. As difficult as it is, I choose to respect that choice.

Yes, I want to share the wonders of clean water and excellent food choices. I want to talk and talk and talk about the ways to heal naturally.

In the end, we have all been given Free Will. It is our choices that make us who we are.

I want and try my very best to live a life of grace and acceptance of others.

That being said, it doesn't make it easier to lose a lifelong friend, a friend who made my world a lovely place to land.

Until we meet again.

I miss you Kathie.

> "The most beautiful discovery true friends make is that they can grow separately without growing apart."
>
> ELISABETH FOLEY

My Better Half

Being a support person for someone diagnosed with cancer is an amazing job. To be charged with doing everything possible so that another person, in this case one you love dearly, can thrive and be healthy is truly a labor of love. Will there be times when you are tired and don't feel up to the task? Of course, after all we're all human and have limitations. Will there be times when you question whether what you are doing makes a difference? Probably, as the results are often not readily apparent. But you do your best and then try to do a little more!

I've had the privilege of being the officiant at many weddings. It's a genuine joy for me to see the love, the affection, and the joy on a couple's faces when they say the magical words "I do". Even during our "enlightened" age, many couples still want to say the words "...in sickness and health, for richer or for poorer" and so on. I honestly believe few ever stop to contemplate the meaning behind "in sickness and in health." A commitment is just that: a promise to follow through. It's easy enough when everyone is healthy and vibrant, but the day will come when that commitment will be put to the test. Sadly, we've had more than a couple of friends and acquaintances tell us they don't believe their spouse would be there for them if they were diagnosed with cancer. Really? I always want to ask why they are with that person, but of course there might be other reasons, although I can't imagine any that are that important compared to helping the one you love.

"Look for the helpers..."

MR. FRED ROGERS

I spent 18 years as an out-patient mental health counselor and have heard so many people utter the phrase "it's not fair ..." and then fill in the blank. Fair is not automatic in life and let's be real, fair is determined individually. When Daleen was diagnosed with cancer, it would have been easy to say that was not fair. Be cautious of those thoughts, for they are filled with presumptions that life should be or is fair. If you live your life thinking you should only have things happen to you that are fair, then you will be sorely disappointed. You will also become bitter and in some cases even caustic. Life simply is not fair, but rather life is to be experienced! Your life as a support person will be filled with challenges and opportunity. Will you be tired one day when the person you support is a challenge? Of course, you will. That's when you remember your role, which is to be there and do what you can for the person you support.

Back to the day Daleen was told she had cancer, a truly ugly day. Fast forward to the day when Daleen decided to say no to chemotherapy and radiation. That day I was in the dark. Daleen had determined a path about which I knew nothing. I was ignorant about cancer, treatment of cancer and actually anything about cancer. Was Daleen making the right choice? Despite my ignorance, I knew my role – to support her in every and any way possible. When time permitted I quickly learned the horrifying facts about what happens to people when they climb aboard the cancer train. I was determined to help Daleen get off of that train and to get well naturally.

I'm a schedule guy. I enjoy consistency and the knowledge of how a day will unfold. That stated, even at my age I don't think I've ever had a day go precisely as planned or expected. It is the same when you think about being a support person. Your needs, while important, become secondary for the most part. Have no fear, your needs will eventually be addressed. The person you support is the focus.

> **"We are not here to fix, change or belittle another person.**
> **We are here to support, forgive and heal one another."**
>
> MARIANNE WILLLIAMSON

After that first awful day, to say the days after were tumultuous would do a disservice to that word. Her world was in upheaval; fear was pervasive, and anxiety ruled the day. My role, and the role of every support person, was to be the even keel, the steady person on who Daleen could rely. Schedules were created, routines established, and life went forward. We changed everything many times along the way. During those first few days and weeks, my role was the organizer. I created spreadsheets for appointments, things to do, places to go. Then as time went on up to the day when Daleen decided that a more natural path was the way for her to go, being supportive was relatively simple. Wake up, do the chores, even the ones she normally did, and look at the spreadsheet to see what was ahead for that day. But after choosing a natural, gentle pathway, suddenly being a support person meant I had to learn. I had to read, read, and then read some more. I learned that the woman I wed long ago was stronger and more determined than I realized. Daleen has always been determined, but I also saw an incredible strength and a firm resolve towards good health. That strength and resolve would be put to the test immediately during her last visit to her oncologist when she announced, "no chemotherapy, no radiation." Being a support person means that you provide the shoulder to cry on when needed and an unwavering dedication to making things as smoothly as possible. The first few weeks were overwhelming in terms of learning. There was so much we didn't know about cancer and how to treat it naturally. We made multiple weekly trips to the library and learning how to differentiate opinion from fact with information gathered from the internet. Daleen is a copious note-taker, but usually on whatever material is handy at the time: post it notes, napkins, ripped pieces of paper, 3x5 cards – you get the idea. Organizing some of her writings was a challenge but there was so much to learn from so many amazing people. Along the way, we discovered that many had trod down the same path we were on, and that knowledge was a source of hope and strength.

Remember when I said I'm a schedule guy? Some days the schedule got tossed in the trash and we reacted. My job was easy, it was to sometimes say nothing more than "Sure, let's give that a whirl" or "what do we have to lose?" Some days my job was to find the money to try what Daleen was thinking would be a good idea. I rarely say no and keep the words "Hurts none, help some" on my mind when saying "Yes, that's a good idea." Turns out, most have been good ideas. Some far better than others but all the while we were secure in the knowledge that the current idea might not be THE answer, but the next one could, and the cumulative effect could be nothing but positive.

> ## "Your support network is the solid ground from which you can propel yourself upwards"
>
> ANNA BARNES

Eventually, the idea that you are the support person gradually fades as what was once upheaval now becomes routine. Now my role as a support person has generally evolved into freeing up time for Daleen so she can stay focused on whatever she's learning or doing. Oh sure, I still say yes, "We'll find the money somewhere" and learned that for people dealing with cancer, a budget is a guide, not a rule.

A word here about choosing to walk down a natural healing path. Your insurance will pay for next to nothing. In these great United States, insurance companies will gladly pay to fix and repair, but seldom pay to prevent and maintain. Re-building and maintaining your immune system is something everyone should do, but insurance companies will not help. If your immune system is failing you and bad things happen, then the insurance companies will pay to apply remedies. If that seems backwards to you, it is because it's the precise opposite of how it should work. Prescriptions are paid for, buying supplements and vitamins will not be reimbursed. They'll pay to have lymph nodes removed, but not for a Rebound-Air to get the lymphatic system working in the first place. Sigh. There is so much wrong with the insurance system in America!

If I was forced to sum up what being a support person is in a few words, I'd have to say that it means nothing more than being there for whoever you support. In mind and body. You've had many roles to play in life, being a support person is simply another role to master.

Gentle Suggestion

Embrace the role of being a support person; you were given it for a reason!

Jump for your Life!

Growing up we had a playground fort in our backyard. You had to climb up a dozen stairs to reach to the clubhouse. In addition to having lunch and playing with Barbies, my sisters and I would write or color in secret diaries, read, play house and of course decorate with found leaves, flowers and branches. Our youngest sister would make us "soup" with water from the hose and freshly picked chives. We ate a lot of chive soup.

If you didn't want to go back down the ladder, there was a thick scratchy rope with knots in it to climb down. Sometimes we would put a blanket on the grass under the tower and when we went down the rope, the other sisters would yell at the top of their lungs, **"JUMP FOR YOUR LIFE"**! The object was not to touch the grass "or hot molten lava field" as we referred to it. Can you tell, we grew up in the shadow of a volcano?

That EXCELLENT advice has followed me for more than 50 years. Believe it or not, it has saved my life and I am here to tell you, it can help save your vibrant life as well.

One of my regrets throughout this journey was not giving myself time to study each thing I did not understand before I allowed the doctors to perform surgery.

I was not told, nor was it part of the discussion that they might be removing lymph nodes as part of the surgery. "Allowing" them to take out 4 lymph nodes was not in the best interest of my health.

"We removed four Lymph nodes; sent them away for analysis, got the results back and we found cancer in them."

Thanks for doing that.

WAIT! WHAT?

Within our Lymphatic system, our Lymph nodes are **SUPPOSED** to clean out all sorts of garbage including broken cells, waste products, bacteria and other damaged cancerous cells if present and remove them from our bodies. *My Lymph nodes were working and doing their job!!!*

Ever see a mom gently rock a baby seated in a grocery cart? Have you ever seen a senior citizen rock in a rocking chair? How about watching a person who jumps on a Rebound-Air every day, or those amazing girls who jump rope at the speed of lightening? Movement *jump starts* our Lymphatic system makes it function properly. Our Lymph nodes **HELP** us stay healthy. When they are removed..... where does the garbage go? How does our body work to remove toxins and dead cells from our system?

The Lymphatic system does not function well, unless we make it move and help it do its job. A healthy, vital, lymphatic system works by expansion and contraction of your muscles to move it around your body and eliminate waste.

Today, each of the (Dr. Joanna) Budwig Clinics has a Rebound-Air in every one of their guest hotel rooms. Yes, it is that vital and important to help our lymphatic system remove waste.

My Rebound-Air www.rebound-air.com has been instrumental in cleaning out toxins from my body. It also improves my circulation, cardiovascular system, strengthens my lower leg muscles, increases oxygen, improves my immune system and helps my balance and posture. I happily use it every day. Sometimes, I even take it outdoors and jump in the sunshine. I whole heartedly recommend buying a rebound-air. If you cannot afford it, start an envelope. Put five dollars in there today and start saving.

While you are saving up for a Rebound-air, for less than $10.00 you can buy a jump rope. The up and down motion is the exact same motion to help our lymphatic system function better. In addition to all the health benefits of rebounding, using a jump rope helps hone your flexibility.

After surgery my balance was off. I put the Rebound-air near a doorway so I could steady myself. However, they do sell a bar to add on if you need a bit more stability. You might say, oh, I can't jump because of a sprained ankle, hurt knee etc. Sit on it and bounce up and down. It works. One other suggestion is to buy some socks with the grippy dots on the bottom. While you get use to jumping happily, you won't accidently slip and the socks also give you a bit of confidence.

You might enjoy looking into the international club and online presences of www.40plusdoubledutchclub.org. The women are incredible and offer up inspiration with sassy encouragement along with top notch abilities. If they don't inspire you, I don't know what will.

There is also an American Jump Rope National Championship. www.amjrf.com Every single one of these athletes is unbelievably talented. You will be smiling the entire time you watch any video of them. You will be inspired.

Gentle Suggestion

Jump for your life!

Bare Footin'

Each year at the beginning of summer, my sisters and I would each get a new pair of leather Salt Water Sandals. Like clockwork, at the end of each day, my mother would always ask how our feet got so dirty. The simple answer was, we would bend our sandals and slip our feet out of them. The ankle strap would still be in use, except the sandals were flapping behind us. Apparently, less work than bending down and taking off our sandals?

We loved to go barefoot. Even when we had to hop, skip and jump across sharp gravel, beach rocks or hot pavement, we loved the feel of our feet on the earth.

At some point after growing up, I stopped going barefoot with the exception of walking inside our home and the occasional day beach combing.

Since the 1960's manufacturers have stopped making our shoes with leather soles. Since that time, our health as a nation has declined. We all wear shoes made out of plastic. We are not connecting with Mother Earth.

Nature is the secret to healing.

One-fifth of the world's population never wears shoes – ever!

Earthing, also known as Grounding.

"<u>Earthing, The Most Important Health Discovery Ever</u>" by Clinton Ober, Stephen T. Sinatra, MD., Martin Zucker This book is inspiring, well researched and I can say, the ultimate source for health and healing.

"<u>The Earth Prescription</u>" by Laura Koniver, MD. This book is full to overflowing with simple ways to incorporate grounding practices every day, every season. She offers common sense ideas and the research to back it up.

Have you ever experienced jet lag? Find a patch of grass, take off your shoes and socks and spend 15 minutes becoming grounded.

Did you have trouble sleeping last night? Oops, did you forget to do your grounding yesterday?

But wait, there's more...

Have you ever had one of those behind the eye, nagging ever so slightly headaches? Take off your shoes and walk on the earth.

Are you feeling a bit stressed about an upcoming huge presentation? Take off those expensive high heels or polished Italian loafers and walk on some grass. You will be amazed at how much more grounded you feel after just a few minutes.

All for the LOW, LOW price of **FREE!**

Grounding/Earthing is like hitting the re-set button for your body.

Try walking barefoot on the earth, in the grass, on the beach, in your backyard, at a rest stop, wherever you can find earth. Sleep on a grounding mat. We do. Wear flip flops or shoes that have copper in the souls to facilitate you grounding. I love my flip-flops. I also have a grounding mat that I use when I stitch or type. I am grounded as I type.

I like to have my morning coffee outdoors, wondering around our garden. Our dog and I each are barefoot. Sometimes, I snap a picture. It makes me smile.

Gentle Suggestion

Right this very minute, slip off your fancy red cowgirl boots, your well-balanced sneakers, or your Salt Water Sandals. Let your tootsies breathe. Find some earth.

Start dancing again with Mother Nature. You are worth it.

Sleep Well

According to IMS Health about 59 million sleeping pill prescriptions were filled in America in 2012.

6 out of 10 Americans report having insomnia a few nights a week.

The National Sleep Foundation reveals 70 million people in the USA have sleeping disorders.

As the saying goes, "Houston, we have a problem".

During sleep your body works to repair muscles, organs and other cells. Chemicals that strengthen your immune system start to circulate in your blood. During sleep, cells in the body produce proteins – the building blocks to form new cells needed during...wait for it...**the healing process.**

Good quality, deep, reparative sleep is beneficial for your health and wellness.

> **"Sleep is like a golden chain that binds our health and our body together."**
>
> THOMAS DEKKER

Excellent sleep increases blood flow, releases healing hormones, reduces inflammation and provides energy for repair. Surgery, illness or injuries are all stressful events. Sleep relieves stress.

Stress depletes magnesium and magnesium relieves stress. Dr. Mark Sircus teaches us that magnesium allows the muscles to relax providing a calming effect that allows for deeper relaxation and better sleep. He has written several excellent, well written, informative books regarding health. Dr. Sircus' book on Magnesium is enlightening and helpful.

Author Dave Asprey's book, <u>Super Human</u> is full of practical help when it comes to how sleep affects our health, energy levels, focus and longevity. He shares 20 plus years of research.

Even if you think you are in tip-top shape, sleep like a baby, do not need any help or advice in getting a better night's sleep, then maybe this next statement will pique your interest.

"Sleep is also incredibly important for warding off Alzheimer's disease, the killer many of us fear most as aging begins its silent creep. When you are asleep, your brain undergoes a natural detoxification process…flushes out cellular waste and neurotoxins." Mr. Asprey also shares two sentences that are worth writing down. "Sleep is the ultimate tool to sharpen every skill and add more quality years to your life. So get better at it."

To facilitate healing and better overall health, I have intentionally set about figuring out how to sleep better.

"Sleep Perchance to Dream"

WILLIAM SHAKESPEARE

We can all agree that quality sleep is beneficial for healing. Spending time researching, learning and implementing any or all of the following suggestions is worthy of our time.

To get better sleep, here are some things I tried, use and maybe your health could benefit from several of them as well.

Surprise! I am sharing another list of Practical Hope for you!

Establish a routine: go to bed at the same time each night

Daily grounding/earthing

Sleep on a mattress covered with a grounding mat

Eat 1 teaspoon raw honey, 30 minutes before bed

Starting at 8:00 pm, dim all the lights in your home

Unplug the computer Wi-Fi router each night

Add Moringa seeds

Use a Bio-mat, at some point during the day

Stop all Fluoride

Unplug all unnecessary electrical devices in your bedroom

Wear a sleep mask

Buy a new mattress, and regularly vacuum your existing mattress

Journaling before bed to settle your brain

Leave cell phone in another room

Sleep on a Silverite pillow

Dry brush your body daily

Drink Clove tea

Open windows, 20 minutes each day, to clean out the air

Use essential oils such as Lavender and Vetiver

Shut down all screens two hours before bed

Consider using 100% cotton linens

Upon waking, get 3 minutes of direct sunlight when you can

No sunshine available? Use a Happy Light!

Hours before going to bed, turn on salt lamps

Remove all EMF's and electronics from bedroom

Cover all lights, even the tiny smoke detector light

Invest in blackout curtains

Wear 100% cotton pajamas

Sleep in a cool room. 68 -69 degrees seems like the researched sweet spot

To fall asleep faster and sleep longer and wake up fewer times, wear socks to bed.

Deep clean bedroom, vacuum under the bed, wipe down dust

Use detox foot pads, quarterly

Use red lights for bathroom night light

Take a warm bath before bed with Magnesium flakes

Toss out bright white LED and compact fluorescent lights

Use an air purifier to filter air

Take Bio-available Magnesium, it promotes good sleep

Drink Chamomile tea or Golden Milk before bed

No Blue Light after 9pm

Wear Blue Blocker glasses for evening computer work, screens

Change light bulbs near bed to red LED

Try Buteylco Breathing, Breathslim, Dr. Marc Sircus

Gentle Suggestion

Make the effort to sleep well. May your mind rest and your body heal.

Hope Floats

Several years ago, a "friend" thought I was spending too much time at home, alone. She suggested that I consider volunteering. It would be good for me to get out, feel useful and make new friends. It might even boost my health.

Unbeknownst to her, I had been keeping a journal the year prior to her suggestion. I had logged 340 hours of volunteer time.

In addition to volunteering, I kept a sparkling clean house, planted a garden, remembered to send 10 + thoughtful cards a month, made all the gifts we gave, baked & cooked dinner 6 nights a week, took care of our animals and worked a part time job, 4 hours, twice a week job (which, because I was such a "good" worker, morphed into a full time job). I also hosted, and cooked everything from scratch, a yearly formal sit down dinner for 20 people, hosted all the holiday dinners, chaperoned, and drove kids everywhere. We had only one car, when Mr. Right did not bike the 11 miles to work, I dropped him off prior to dropping kids at two different schools, then drove myself to work. Then at the end of the day, I reversed the process, picked everyone up and went on to the soccer, football, drama practice, running, sports our boys were involved in.

I was busy. I sure felt important.

WAIT, what?

Ouch, you read that correctly, by using the word "busy" I felt vital and important.

I was so busy that I could conveniently tuck away all the emotional stuff I didn't want to deal with. Being busy allowed me to say yes to everything! I could and would fit it in. Ask a busy person to teach Sunday school, or bring a hot dish, they will never say no.

> "There is no such thing as work-life balance.
> There are work-life choices, and you make
> them, and they have consequences."

JACK WELCH

I was so busy feeling important and in control that I had never even heard of *White Space.*

White Space is the unscheduled time, to do nothing. Taking time to drink a cup of coffee and read a chapter, not drink coffee in a to-go cup, drinking it while driving to an activity. I was unable to make it a priority to sit still for a moment, long enough to watercolor a small bouquet of flowers or take a luxurious bath. A quick, efficient shower, after which I tidied up the bathroom and put out fresh towels and did a quick clean up of the sink area was my usual routine.

My lack of health required me to exchange the word busy for the word balance.

Every time I would glimpse a magazine picture of a beautiful bubble bath with candles, and soft lighting, river rocks on the ledge and foamy bubbles, I thought how luxurious. I secretly wanted that, yet, my unhealthy brain would have me think it was a waste of time. I had too many things on the schedule.

There were things to do, places to go, volunteer hours to add up!

Fast forward on figuring out how I got so sick and how was I going to get myself out of this mess.

As luck would have it, Mr. Right had joined a chess club that met once a week on Wednesday nights.

This got me thinking, you know, maybe, I should mark the calendar and "schedule" a two hour bubble bath every single week?

I purchased battery operated candles and essential oils that I adored. I searched for and finally found non toxic bubble bath (Alafia) which was trickier than you might think. I chose lovely music, a goblet for some ice water; I also splurged on new fluffy, cotton towels. The order of the day was to make my Jacuzzi spa tub magazine worthy. I was taking steps and learning how to make my health a priority.

On the cover of Mark Sloan's book, <u>Bath Bombs & Balneotherapy</u>, it reads "The surprising health benefits of bath bombs, ancient secrets of hot springs, dead sea minerals, carbon dioxide baths for disease treatment".

I had my next research topic right in front of me.

Nafis Kahn at the Vermont Salt Cave Halotherapy Center in Montgomery Center, Vermont, taught me about using 35% hydrogen peroxide in my baths. From Dr. Mark Sircus I explored and learned so much about magnesium flakes and baking soda and how they help to heal the body. Dead Sea Minerals, healing essential oils, raising the water temperature high enough to create the perfect environment for healing all were part and parcel to creating an amazing, luxurious, healing experience.

"If there is magic on this planet it is contained in water."

LOREN EISELEY

The summer of 2023, Mr. Right and I made a pilgrimage to Soap Lake. Compared to the ocean and other known naturally occurring mineral resources in the world, Soap Lake has the highest diverse mineral content of any body of water *on the planet!* Soap Lake water also contains ichthyols, an oil-like substance sold over the counter in Europe to treat infections and abrasions.

This particular lake contains 23 minerals and is highly alkaline with a pH of 9.8. Similar to the Dead Sea in Israel and Jordan, Soap Lake is dense and buoyant, allowing swimmers to float easily.

On the summer day while we were soaking in the lake with 14 other people, the temperature was 97° Fahrenheit and we were the only two who were speaking English. Does it seem that folks from European countries value and embrace the idea of natural healing through minerals and water more so than their American counter parts?

In the early 1900's the town of Soap Lake was a boom town including hotels, spas, cabins, resorts, restaurants, shops and by the looks of photos, people. Many people had traveled far distances to take part, bring sick and ill family members to benefit from the healing waters.

Today, Soap Lake is a quiet, one gas station town. It feels sad and uninviting despite having 1,700 souls who call it home. Where are the visitors? *Is everyone healed and healthy?* It is located 134 miles from Seattle, Washington. Why did people stop visiting? Why don't people want to use the mud for health and wellness? When did we become so jaded and turn away from the healing powers of Mother Nature? When did our belief in pharmaceuticals trump the belief and power of nature? Have we experienced better results with manmade drugs? People are willing to fly several states away to visit a mouse and are more than willing to save and fly to another country to have dental and medical work done. Yet, to heal themselves or family members, they are neither interested nor curious enough to drive less than 3 hours to experience healing. There are miracles around us, sometimes; many wellness answers are right in front of our noses.

While on your travels throughout America you might consider experiencing the healing waters in the village of Elkhart Lake, Wisconsin, and the Omni Homestead Resort (founded in 1766) in Hot Springs, Virginia or Pagosa Springs, Colorado. Stay curious and in awe of the magnificent healing power of nature.

Bathing can be a remarkable healing journey. I am always giddy when I see the magazine worthy bath tub area I have created. Together with the boat load of science and knowledge, somehow with soft lighting and calm music I am transported into a meditative state. Deep below the glorious bubbles the water holds healing properties.

Another Practical Hope list headed your way:

Improve your immune system to be better able to fight off viruses

Balance hormones

Reduce pain and inflammation

Calm the nervous system

Help with breathing

Hydrate the body

Rejuvenate body and mind

Facilitate better sleep

Lower blood pressure and support heart health

Reduce stress and anxiety

Increase your oxygen

I have traded the word busy for the word balanced. It does not come naturally. I have to practice and make the effort. I am worthy of the process.

Gentle Suggestion

Stay curious and in awe of the magnificent power of water.

Make the effort to create a beautiful bathing experience.

You are worthy of healing through water.

Tip the Balance

Once it was determined that I had a serious illness, I had a Lou-Lou of a time finding balance. Full disclosure: I still work at creating balance on a daily basis. While recovering and finding wellness, I still had to go about my daily life. It's really a dance. It's two days forward and one day back. Cha cha cha!

We have all heard the motto, "Live each day like it is your last." On the surface that may seem like sound advice, however, it is also a HUGE, almost unattainable, goal to set about fulfilling. It feels like a heavy burden. No one wants to have their last day filled with scrubbing grout or grocery shopping. Yet this still needs your attention. This might be my last Thanksgiving; I better bake my famous Pumpkin pie one last time. Grudgingly, someone has to take out the garbage, pay a bill and fold the laundry. To follow the "live each day" motto is quite simply *exhausting*.

While I am always grateful, for another day, in my mind it sometimes seems I should be glowing with gratitude and grace, moving gently about, pleased with everything and everyone. Yet, I am still a normal girl who wants to complain a bit about my hair style, the neighbor shooting off fireworks in June, fuss about paint color and whine about what to make for supper.

I am supremely grateful for walking a path of healing and yes, sometimes I do indeed find the energy to grumble under my breath about having my Budwig Protocol in place of a daily lunch. I am under no illusions that I am fortunate to have the money to pay for the protocol. The stubborn 4th grade girl inside me still complains now and then. It's not pretty, it's just the truth.

How do I tip the balance?

While I am feeling lucky and happily teeter tottering one moment and then bam, my fanny hits the ground, my teeth get a jolt and I need to re-group. I gather some strength to push-off with my feet to send my side of the teeter-totter on the upswing into the clouds.

Recently, while at a grocery store, I lost my balance when my eyes filled with tears as I learned about yet another favorite food that I have to say good-bye to. Crackers that I had enjoyed for years had recently added ingredients that I am choosing to forgo. Even with regularly purchased products many ingredient change so often, label reading for me has become a constant requirement.

There is nothing lofty about cleaning under the sink or re-staining the front porch. I still need to vacuum the car and feed the chickens. News flash, I cannot sit each day, all day long, with my hands folded in prayer of thanksgiving. I can't spend the entire day researching, learning, re-bounding and doing protocols. Some chores require that I get up, pull on my yellow work gloves and accomplish physical work. Hey, that garden hose isn't going to roll itself up.

Balance is a fascinating topic. We all are tickled to find out a business co-worker goes home to his other life and is an accomplished ukulele player. We are in awe of our relative who is an Engineer by trade, yet quietly and amazingly built a gorgeous, huge sailboat in his backyard (with one inch clearance on either side to move it through the fence gate). We are happily surprised to learn when a graphic designer trades her computer for sneakers and runs marathons. When you find out a master gardener with dirt stained hands, is also a mom and concert pianist, you can't help but smile. These people make us feel good. They give us hope. There are the folks among us who have figured it out. They have created balance in their world, and they are healthier because of it.

I continue to heal every single day. However, I do not live on a movie set where I am dressed in a beautiful, embroidered gown and float among everyone being happy and serene and grateful. I still get ticked off by ill mannered folks. I still burn food. Heck yeah, I even cuss now and then. On occasions, I still act like a spoiled child when the "want" platform outweighs the "give" platform.

The book, <u>The Year of Pleasure</u> authored by Elizabeth Berg, helps nudge us in the right direction. "I know you are hurting! But what if you do one thing each day that you enjoy…I know, count your blessings…no, I am not talking about things that happen to you. I am talking about things you make happen. I am talking about purposefully doing one thing that brings you happiness every single day, in a very conscious way. It builds up the arsenal. It tips the balance."

It tips the balance.

I adore that way of thinking.

Instead of feeling sorry for myself, which, truthfully does happen, I look for ways to build up the arsenal. I look for one "happy" a day.

On a Sunday drive, we ended up beside a river. We go exploring. I found a few, somewhat flat rocks and started stacking them. Trying out different rocks that would balance on the rock before it was mesmerizing. In the past, you have possibly come upon someone's rock tower that they balanced. It took time. The person was in the moment. The practice of rock balancing made them happy.

Bliss lies in Balance

Somehow, one day has turned into two and those two days turned into a few months and believe it or not, now and then, I actually forget to count the exact days on the calendar. Side note, yes, as I typed this I can calculate very quickly the years, months and days since, the precise day/moment I fell out of balance.

That jolt of the teeter totter slamming down? That happens when I panic and fret about a sore thumb or small bruise on my toe. Um, no, you are not sick again; maybe it is just a bruise from stubbing your toe on the rocking chair?"

Some days I foolishly spend an extraordinary amount of time wondering if I will get sick again. On those days, I gently remind myself to choose something to do with my hands that will fill up my soul. Taking action sort of breaks the spell of brain swirling. I bake or garden, quilt, ride my bike, cross stitch, paint, or sew. I make an effort to tip the balance.

Making the effort to control the balance brings about happiness.

I look for beautiful leaves.

I try a new recipe.

Spend time learning to water color paint.

I sew dresses for the grandgirlies in my life.

Currently I am stock piling supplies to make to baseball themed quilts for our two grandsons.

For some reason buying funny socks for Mr. Right and seeing my guy dressed in "go to work" clothes while knowing he has on goofy socks, makes me chortle.

Just for happiness, every Saturday for a year, I traded pictures of eating a banana with grand #3. We each ate a banana and then traded pictures. **This is HAPPINESS pure and simple.** It makes me happy to see his picture and he gets to yell, Grandma, Banana! (His parents are happy that they got a toddler to eat something.)

While on a walk, I found a gigantic Maple leaf and it made me happy. Golly, a leaf as big as my head? I *had* to share a picture with my grands.

Even on the crummy days, I continue to look for one happy.

On my daily search, I have stumbled upon, gigantic leaves, banana pictures, sweet dresses, flowers for my bicycle basket, giving my chickens frozen peas on a hot day, using colored pencils, buying organic sprinkles, making a flower arrangement from my back yard flowers, buying colorful buttons and yes, goofy socks.

The crummy, tears dripping, scary, painful, uncertain, loud, ugly, frustrating, brain swirling days still surface now and again, and by golly, my arsenal is full to over flowing. I can choose any amount of happy I need to recall. It all balances out.

Gentle Suggestion

"Balance is not something you find.
It is something you create."

JANA KINGSFORD

Water

Before I share "the list", I am going to expand on one of the items. The rest of the list will be extremely simplified. You will get to deep dive into each one and explore your own list of changes for better health.

"Pure water is the first and most important medicine in the world."

SLOVAKIAN PROVERB

Not the pitcher in your refrigerator that makes water taste and smell better. Not the filtered water and ice cubes you get by pushing a button on the outside door of your expensive refrigerator. By the way, when was the last time you cleaned that line and replaced the filter? What does it filter out? The bottled water from your very nice grocery store, in the *plastic* bottle that has been sitting in the heat and cold of your car, is not what I am talking about. Yes, your town mails to each resident a beautiful glossy brochure touting your water is the best. Yes, I understand you live in a gated community and you have only the "best water". If by "best" tap water, you actually mean recycled waste water...I will wait and let that sink in. Yes, recycled waste water. Water that contains plastics, fertilizers, carcinogenic Glyphosate – "Round –Up", carcinogenic Fluoride, pharmaceutical medicine, toxic Chlorine, Lead, Mercury, Chromium (not the good kind, the kind from industrial waste), and the list of undesirables goes on and on. I think you are smart enough that I do not need to expand the list to include some very undesirable things that are in our water supply.

In each of our communities, originally when developing water treatment plants, they were assigned the job of stopping Cholera and Dysentery. Now they have to add Chlorine to combat some unpleasant and toxic wastes.

You can check your tap water by going to ewg.org/tap water. Type in your state and zip code and you will discover more useful information. The town in which I currently live has 768X the amount of Arsenic in which the ewg.org reports is okay. Very few of us are exempt from water contamination. Put your detective hat back on and please do your due diligence.

Mike Adams, www.healthranger.com has done extensive research on clean water. He has discovered and documented that at least 75% of all American households have some type of contaminated water.

Remember to ask yourself, who funded the research before you start boasting about your water supply.

You can simply ask the folks who live in Flint, Michigan or East Palestine, Ohio if clean water is important. Why do people pack their suitcases with bottles of water on their vacations to foreign countries? Ask yourself, why do Delta Force soldiers carry their own personal Skatadyn water filter/purifier, made in Switzerland? (These are very pricey, at the time of this writing about $400.00 each.) One reason might be, no matter how brave, fierce, intelligent, bad-ass, that you are, CLEAN water is the great equalizer. We cannot live a healthy, vital, clear processing / thinking life without clean water.

> "There's a very fundamental basic value system that I think America was built upon, and that's mutual respect, honor, integrity and concern for our environment and the right to clean water. And we have moved away from it."
>
> ERIN BROCKOVICH

Troy Casey, www.certifiedhealthnut.com reminds us, humans are 70% water. Our brains are about 90% water. The purity of water is extremely important. The quality of life you live is directly related to the food and water you ingest.

Are you looking for fresh, clean spring water near you? You can fill your own glass containers, just by typing in your location. www.findaspring.com

Please put forth the effort and learn about clean water. After many hours of research, for the time being we have settled on the Berkey Water filter system. We then structure that water. Then we turn our structured water into Hydrogenated water.

We decided the Berkey water system would work well for our home and family. Pay attention to the water that is being used in your home. We have two adults, one large dog, cooking, showering, water color painting (yes, chemicals in the water change the paint colors slightly), chickens, a garden, watering indoor plants, ironing etc., so the size and filters of the Berkey system seem to be a good fit for our needs.

Side notes: Ever wonder why so many pets today have such horrid issues with their kidneys? Are you filling their water bowls with top quality purified water?

Once you source and are using your **clean** water, please make the effort to learn about putting back in minerals and real salt that our bodies need.

Please consider taking some time and read about clean water. You, your family and pets are worth it (or not, your choice, remember no judgment)... Berkey Water filters, ionized water, reverse osmosis, structured water, Hydrogen water etc...make an informed decision and figure out what will work best for you. As of this writing, we continue to learn. We are researching a filter to use outdoors to water our garden.

Gentle Suggestion

Source the best water you can without going neurotic. Buy a water filter system that you can afford and start saving up for the next level of clean water, today. If you don't have an excellent water filter, YOU are the water filter.

The List

When I mention healing, wellness and my book, the conversation inevitably ends up with two words, "The List".

From the beginning of my healing journey, I needed to be a detective and figure out what I was doing wrong to cause my cells not to function properly. What things do I toss aside, which things do I tweak a bit and which things have to be stomped in the backyard while wearing Mr. Right's old Army boots?

To switch my health from poor to thriving, we started keeping a list of all the changes we made.

I understand that not every single action, product or the absence of something was going to bring about complete and total healing. However, for a more positive outcome, I had to make the effort towards better, overall healthier choices.

Please close your eyes for a moment (only a moment or you won't be able to continue reading) and imagine Lady Justice and her scales in particular. She holds those scales in her right hand. The metal piece that holds the two pans are attached to chains. The scales are empty and hang precisely even.

I have pictured her more times than I can count.

I need those scales to be tipped in MY favor. I need one side to be piled high with healing ideas, products, books, tips, suggestions and hope. I NEED one pan to be overflowing with all the things that will heal, help me recover, thrive and ground my wellness. I also need one of the pans to be empty and flying high.

> **"If you do not change direction, you might end up where you are heading."**
>
> LAO TZU

Each change is listed once. While in reality I bought and paid for nine different deodorants over time to test what worked best for me, I only wrote that change once. I had to experiment with several different make up products, again, I only wrote it down once.

The list is daunting. The list is hard, tricky, expensive, boring, not popular, difficult, sometimes tastes bad and at times, not fun. Yet every single change will (extract from you) your time and commitment to health and overall wellness. Every single item is change.

Change is hard.

I need to see progress. In my mind, I want to visualize the overflowing scale in my favor. When I look at the many things I have changed, I have a pretty good feeling they are positive changes. On occasion when I feel like nothing is working, all I have to do is sit down and actually read the list. By reading through some of my choices, I am splashing myself with the grace and goodness that I have chosen and collectively these things are adding up to health & vitality.

Some items or actions on the list are free, they cost nothing. Some items are a pricey date. You might have to save up. Mark an envelope right now, I will wait. On the outside of the envelope, print in big, glorious, bold letters, "HEALTH AND WELLNESS". Make a commitment to add money every week or every paycheck. May I gently suggest you put a five dollar bill in the envelope today? Plant the seed money. You are worth health and wellness! When the time comes and you want to buy a great healing book or program, the money will be there. When you decide it is time to buy a Rebound- Air, your envelope will be waiting. That non- toxic lipstick you learned about....yes, indeed, go to the envelope and take out some wellness money.

For over 10 years, I have studied 1 hour a day, 5 days a week, 11 months of the year.

While I have read about and researched each of the items, I have no idea how to share my stack of spiral notebooks filled to overflowing with research notes and thus offering evidence that they work. Each change is working, that is what matters to me.

Some of the items listed might make you mad, cause you to disagree or even get your dander up; this is where that beautiful thing called *Free Will* comes in. This is where you should do your own research, question, dig a little and find the reasons behind my choices, then and only then should you consider making healthy changes for you.

There are over 200 items on my list. That number changes with each new thing we learn and implement. I continue to research, learn, grow, change, all aiming towards vibrant health.

"The Power to Heal is Yours"

ROBERT SCOTT BELL

Most items on the list will be direct and to the point. I will share book titles, and company names & websites for any practical help in separate lists.

There is one exception, *water*. In fact, because of the importance, the chapter prior to this list will be dedicated to **Drinking Clean Water.**

Buckle up, friend, it could get bumpy.

This is my list.

1. Have a steadfast belief in a higher power, tap into that power.
2. Drink clean water.
3. Sincerely forgive who you need to. Forgive, Forgive, and Forgive.
4. Make a list of the items that contributed to your cancer.
5. Listen daily to Wholetones. www.wholetones.com
6. Eat an organic radish everyday.
7. Purchase 100% untreated cotton pajamas.
8. Purchase 100% untreated cotton sheets and pillowcases.
9. Stop using all sunscreen. www.primallypure.com
10. Buy only natural, organic hand-made soaps.
11. Learn to make bar soap.
12. Learn to limit stress.
13. No cell phone before 9 am or after 9 pm.

14. Use all natural fiber pillows.

15. Stop using all herbicides or pesticides on the garden and lawn.

16. Make a photo ring to focus on during stress times.

17. Remove all social media that does not serve me well.

18. Stay away from or remove toxic people from my life.

19. Study 1 hour a day, 5 days a week, 11 months a year.

20. Keep a jar of daily gratitude notes, read on New Year's Eve.

21. Grounding/Earthing every single day of the year.

22. Dry brushing, entire body, towards the heart.

23. Use a washcloth, daily over the biggest organ of your body: your skin.

24. Stay away from unfermented soy.

25. Drink fresh made juice daily.

26. Drink more seltzer water.

27. Drink, white, green, milk thistle or chaga tea daily.

28. Find tea with NO Lead.

29. Eat broccoli sprouts.

30. Use broccoli in your juice daily.

31. Eat apricot seeds for vitamin B17.

32. Learn about & grow your own sprouts.

33. Be of some help or service every single day.

34. Eat berries daily.

35. Eat cooked or dehydrated mushrooms daily.

36. Eat nori daily.

37. Eat one Brazil nut daily for the Selenium.

38. Eat non-GMO oatmeal.

39. Use pure maple syrup.

40. Try a daily snack of apple slices and homemade peanut butter.

41. Embrace sage and other good luck charms.

42. Make and use colorful, cheerful, uplifting quilts.

43. Angels for protection, they are watching over you, helping you heal.

44. No dairy.

45. No laundry detergent, use laundry balls instead, or make your own.

46. Purchase an air filter system such as the Air Doctor.

47. Severely limit white sugar.

48. Get a massage.

49. Whenever possible, take in one hour or more of sunshine daily.

50. Keep chickens for organic eggs.

51. Remove all chemical air fresheners, sprays and candles.

52. Remove all light bulbs with mercury.

53. Use a happy light (in the winter) with full spectrum light.

54. Increase use of ginger.

55. Install Berkey fluoride filter in shower.

56. Use Berkey water filter.

57. Use Himalayan salt lamps.

58. Use royal bee jelly.

59. Research about and use essential oils daily.

60. Eat cultured/fermented foods and drinks daily.

61. Avoid plastics.

62. Listen to music daily.

63. Black out curtains in bedroom.

64. Eye sleep mask for bedroom or travel.

65. Make your own nut milk.

66. Make your own ketchup.

67. Make your own teriyaki sauce.

68. Make your own salad dressing.

69. Make smoothies using coconut water from young coconuts.

70. NEVER again touch cash register receipts (thermal paper).

71. No longer purchase deli/luncheon meats with nitrates.

72. No dryer sheets. Use woolen balls for no static cling.

73. Use only organic natural body wash.

74. Use only organic natural facial products and make up.

75. Open windows in house, 20 minutes daily.

76. Read as much information as you can find on healing.

77. Shungite. Use it, wear it, learn about it.

78. Remove all electronics, all EMF's from your bedroom.

79. Remove all High Fructose Corn Syrup and corn syrup solids.

80. Rid your life of objectionable things, use a hammer when possible.

81. Remove Ajax cleaner, replace with Bon Ami.

82. Ride a bike and indoors ride a stationary bike.

83. Remove all commercial toothpaste – no Fluoride and no chemicals.

84. No scanners at airport security, request a pat down.
85. No chemotherapy.
86. No phthalates.
87. Purchase a Scouf: a scarf with a carbon filter for use in airplane travel.
88. No radiation. If you need an x-ray, request a lead blanket.
89. No mammograms. Thermography instead.
90. No alcohol.
91. Begin aroma therapy.
92. Budwig Protocol, 7 years+
93. Use glass straws.
94. Only eat organic wheat.
95. No artificial colorings.
96. No artificial preservatives.
97. No artificial flavorings.
98. Severely limit gluten.
99. Stop all MSG (Monosodium Glutamate).
100. Stop eating peanuts as some have a fungus.
101. Stop visits to nail salons.
102. Stop putting gas in car, or stand upwind of gas fumes.
103. Throw out microwave oven.
104. Stop putting perfume on skin, instead spray on scarf or blouse.
105. Take Spirulina.
106. Switch to a deodorant with NO aluminum or harmful chemicals.
107. Eat local raw honey.
108. Switch to a non plastic shower curtain.
109. Switch personal products to natural, with no chemicals.
110. Use straws for all juice. Choose a no straw day for good bacteria.
111. Take Iodine six days a week.
112. Baking soda, Magnesium Flake, 35% food grade hydrogen peroxide in baths.
113. Take Barley Max daily. www.mydiet.com
114. Take Bio-available supplements: Copper, Boron, Selenium, etc.
115. Use 35% food grade Hydrogen Peroxide, 3 drops in juice or water, daily.
116. Brush, feed and walk your pet daily.
117. Take Chlorella.

118. Take high doses of vitamin C.
119. Take Magnesium, Calcium before bed.
120. Use Vetiver essential oil on feet prior to bed to calm and stay asleep.
121. Try a weighted blanket for better sleep.
122. Take Bio-available minerals.
123. Take mushroom supplements.
124. Take supplements 6 days a week, one day rest, reboot system.
125. Toast your own raw almonds.
126. Laugh more, watch a video or listen to podcast.
127. Buy and use a Bio-Mat. www.biomats.com
128. No sodium laurel sulfates or sodium laurel sulfites.
129. Use almond oil.
130. Use Frankincense, daily.
131. Use amethyst crystals for healing.
132. Utilize castor oil packs for aches and pains.
133. Choose coconut cream in coffee.
134. Coconut sugar in coffee.
135. Buy organic popcorn.
136. Use natural Aloe Vera.
137. Purchase natural nail polish.
138. Buy natural sweetener products made with fruit.
139. Select natural dish soap or use gloves.
140. Choose organic coconut oil when making popcorn.
141. Use organic, baby bubble bath.
142. Use PH strips, test regularly.
143. Increase use of celery, parsley and carrots.
144. Use shampoo & conditioner with no harmful chemicals.
145. Try bar shampoo.
146. Use trace mineral drops in juice or water.
147. Use speaker only while using cell phone.
148. Write negative thoughts down then burn the paper.
149. Reduce iron supplementation.
150. Increase bio-available copper.
151. Breathe fresh air daily.
152. Build immune system daily.

153. Walk barefoot in the ocean.

154. Surround yourself with nature, trees.

155. Eat pickled vegetables.

156. Make your own weed killer.

157. Plant a garden, grow food, and get dirty.

158. Start a compost pile.

159. Eat black raspberries, dehydrated.

160. Change to all natural healing ointments and first aid.

161. No television or computer after 9 pm.

162. Avoid fried foods.

163. No over cooked, charred food or BBQ.

164. Buy organic natural sprinkles.

165. Dead Sea Minerals for bath.

166. Purchase and use daily a Rebound-Air.

167. Use only fresh lemons, nothing from a bottle.

168. Methylene Blue.

169. Red Light Therapy.

170. Nebulizer with silver.

171. Make structured water.

172. Target shooting for stress relief.

173. Roll on Arnica for aches and pains.

174. CBD cream on joints and knee pain.

175. Purchase certified organic oats.

176. Change all passwords to positive words. (ie. I am Healthy)

177. Grounding mat to sleep on.

178. Grounding mat to put feet on while typing, stitching, sewing etc.

179. No Bio–engineered foods.

180. Make and use bath bombs for the Carbon Dioxide.

181. Make and eat miso soup daily.

182. Add savory ingredients to organic oatmeal.

183. Use apple cider vinegar daily.

184. Use tooth minerals in place of commercial tooth paste.

185. Use dehydrated chaga to warm beverages.

186. Eat an orange daily.

187. Use coconut oil in place of lesser quality oil.

188. Do your research. Listen to many. Trust no one. Verify.

189. Use Silver Hydrosol for first aid.
190. Purchase a newer home. No mold and mildew.
191. Reduce inflammation.
192. Replace metal tea pot with a ceramic one.
193. Lift weights 6 days a week.
194. Use elastic exercise bands.
195. Rosemary oil and water for thinning hair.
196. Wear Blue Tiger Eye, Amber, Amethyst, Shungite necklace/ bracelet, healing jewelry.
197. Buy mill grinder and mill your own flour.
198. Use citronella stickers on clothing, instead of chemicals on skin.
199. No aluminum in baking soda.
200. Use Lemon oil in place of polish to clean wood furniture.
201. Learn to do your own manicure/pedicure.
202. Extremely limit dry cleaning, refuse plastic bag and air out in garage.
203. Make own peanut butter.
204. Buy and use canner.
205. Buy and use dehydrator.
206. Use detox foot pads.
207. Willow Bark tea, in place of aspirin.
208. Do not purchase home on golf course – chemicals.
209. Seek international stores, produce department typically large.
210. Toss out bright white LED and compact fluorescent lights.
211. Unplug unnecessary electrical devices in your house.
212. Reduce blue light exposure at night.
213. Visit a Salt Spa – Halotherapy.
214. No fit bit, or fruit watch: emits non-ionizing RF and EMF radiation.
215. Wear blue light glasses after 9 pm.
216. Gave up television.
217. Drink Golden Milk.
218. Healing with colors.
219. Grow and take Wormwood.
220. Use Comfrey to heal bones (a poultice can heal bone fracture, ask me how I know).
221. Buy and use a Faraday cage.

222. Read all food labels, every time you purchase.
223. Borax for health.
224. Make your own sourdough bread.
225. Stop all seed oils.
226. Use only natural dental floss – no PFAS, no sugar, no fluoride.
227. Make and use People Paste for first aid.
228. Unplug computer Wi-Fi router each night.
229. Never store your phone in your clothing/pocket/or head covering.
230. Learn everything you can about PFAS and how to avoid them at all costs.

Gentle Suggestion

Start your list, today.

Can Backyard Chickens
help you heal?

It was a dark and stormy night…

No, it wasn't.

It was a beautiful, blue sky, warm, sunny June afternoon, 2013.

I was extremely sick. It took effort just to get dressed and put on lipstick. Not the "movie star" kind of sick, the real life, not pretty kind of sick.

My wise, childhood friend was stopping by to visit and bring me something. I was thinking a nice, pretty card or a cheerful bouquet of flowers.

No, wrong guess.

As the agreed upon time approached, I stood looking out our kitchen window. I saw a huge, diesel powered truck pulling a huge horse trailer pull through our circular driveway. I saw my friend in the driver's seat. Along with her were 4 teenagers.

Once the truck stopped and the engine shut off out jumped the teenagers and Kristy. They unloaded a brand new chicken coop, bedding, organic feed, treats, water, feed containers and three young chickens. They carried it all into the backyard and set everything up. (All the while, me babbling and asking questions to my friend.)

While my friend Kristy, smiled a lot, talked about the kids, the weather and having to get going, she climbed back up into the driver's seat. Hurriedly, I passed out ice cold sparkling waters. She started the loud engine. I had to yell to be heard. "I KNOW NOTHING ABOUT RAISING CHICKENS!"

My smiling friend, waved and yelled out her window, "Then I guess you better start learning and fast."

In the same type of whirlwind that they arrived, they left just as quickly. As loud as the truck and commotion was for a few minutes, it was equally deafening in silence.

I walked through the house to the backyard. I stood there with our Golden Retriever, Sweet Liberty, silently looking at 3 small young chickens.

I said to the dog beside me, first order of business, I guess we need to name them?

Ginger, MaryAnn and Lovey Howell.

Okay, now what?

How the heck is this going to work? I know zero about raising chickens. Doesn't she know I am too sick to do this right now? (Unbeknownst to me, she had made a side deal with Mr. Right, if it was too much and didn't work out, she would graciously take them back to her ranch.)

Remember earlier in this chapter, I called her my wise friend?

Somehow, she knew I would have to turn on the computer and read and LEARN. She guessed I would have to get dressed and have Mr. Right drive me to a book store to purchase a couple books on raising chickens. In her smarty, awesome sauce, cowgirl wearing, sparkly belt way, she knew, I would need to get up off the sofa a couple times a day to feed, water, fluff straw, and check on my new animals.

My wise, amazing girlfriend had a feeling that I would need to clean the coop. I would need to carry water, lift bedding, and fill the food container. In the beginning, I was not able to lift a 25 pound bag of bedding or food. From the garden shed to the coop, I had to take many trips with small buckets to refill things.

My wise, thoughtful, beautiful friend from Kindergarten knew that I needed organic eggs to eat. She knew that I needed to be around "farm dirt" and straw and outdoor *good* germs to build back my immune system.

In her wisdom, she knew that to heal, I was going to require feeling grateful, thankful and needed every single day.

Mr. Right only helped when he absolutely needed to. I took care of them myself. I never skipped a day. Some days, while I worked I cried. Other days, I talked to them and worked out "problems". On days when it took me 30 minutes or more to change bedding, straw and give them food and water, just those chores zapped all the energy I had.

A few months later, my little grandgirlie was helping me and she said, "Egg". WHAT??? I couldn't actually believe that we had gotten our first egg! I had to take a picture. One egg, certainly a reason to celebrate!

A week went by and then another. People asked me how many eggs I had collected. I kept track on the calendar. I started sharing pictures. I didn't want the eggs to roll off the counter during the "photo shoot" so... one thing led to another. I started setting the eggs in things. A fruit basket, a creamer shaped like a frog, a bowl full of roasted coffee beans. I used anything I could find.

Here's the update:

I am still counting eggs and taking pictures. In August 2023, I gathered egg number 5, 609.

I am still here, tending my flock.

More chickens have joined the party.

I currently have four chickens. I am healthy enough to lift a bag of bedding. I can walk to the neighbors to share some of my bounty. For several months we donated 20 chicks a month through www.heifer.org. We wanted to donate so others could flourish and thrive, like me.

I continue to be grateful.

I continue to heal and tend to my health.

I continue to raise and tend chickens.

Thanks in part to my friend. Kristy was the friend who believed I could/would do it. She knew that I would get out of bed, put on my snazzy red cowgirl boots and tend to other creatures that needed my help.

I felt needed.

Those chickens need me in the beautiful, blue, sunny skies as well as the blustery, wild wind, cold, pouring rain, snow, and boot wearing, dark stormy days.

Oh, I get it!

My friend was there for me in the dark, stormy days and yes, today on a clear, beautiful day, she is in my corner, celebrating *with me*, over 5,000 gathered eggs.

I am one grateful chick.

Who knew chickens could help me heal?

She did.

Gentle Suggestion

Find something that makes you feel needed every single day.

Health insurance will not pay for your carrots

Years ago, I was helping my cousin prepare for her yearly apple cider pressing party. Lots of family and friends were headed over with boxes and boxes of apples. Each family would take a turn at the press and go home with fresh Apple Cider. The gathering was of course filled with amazing tables of food (indoor and outdoor kitchen) and because of all the fishermen in our family, oodles and oodles of amazing seafood was shared. The big showcase was always the youngsters who preformed for the yearly talent show. Some performed their dance recital routines, some showcased their musical talent and one year our shy, young son performed a magic show. I can still hear the loud roar of cheers after each performance. Each young person gave it their all. They had incentive to bring their "A" game in front of family and friends. Given the opportunity to share their talents, they took full ownership and soared.

As we were preparing the tables, my cousin said she wished she had extra money to buy a huge, gorgeous, magazine worthy centerpiece to showcase all this amazing food.

My mind started swirling and I meandered outside.

It was autumn in the Pacific Northwest, not much "timber" in the way of flowers to make a traditional floral arrangements. I started gathering. Ivy, blackberry and Kiwi vines, twigs, dried gourds, a couple Dahlias still hanging on, paper lantern flowers, apples, curly willow branches, straw flowers in the midst of drying, anything I could find that would lend itself to a beautiful centerpiece. I also found a huge, weathered wooden bucket.

I got to work. I put a plastic bucket inside the wooden one to hold some water. I lost track of time. My cousin came out to see what I was doing.

Before her stood the most amazing, show stopping, glorious riot of color and texture in the form of a stunning centerpiece we had ever seen. She gasped. We hugged. She displayed it in her outdoor kitchen. The sheer size and beauty of the piece somehow elevated the main table laden with even the most mouthwatering of food.

Lack of money, perfectly shaped green house grown flowers and traditional floral arranging supplies did not deter me. In fact, it somehow opened up the opportunity to create something even more outrageous and glorious.

I had incentive.

What could I create? What is there to use?

If you have no incentive, somehow that steals your opportunity to thrive, soar and take full ownership.

One of the phrases I will try to limit repeating, will sound something like this: Let's talk about "health" insurance.

Insurance will not pay for your carrots. Sorry insurance will not pay for yet another book on healing naturally. Oh dear, health insurance will not pay for a Richway Bio-mat or a Rebound-Air, or a Mito Red Light Therapy box, or Chaga for your immune system. It will not pay for new walking sneakers, nor will it pay for spirit lifting Kick-Ass Red Cowgirl boots. I am sorry to be the bearer of bad news, your health insurance will not pay for Black Raspberries from Oregon. Nice try, however, insurance will not pay for a fancy high powered blender nor will it pay for an immersion blender or a Wheat Mill grinder.

Living in America, I am very well acquainted with the idea that you (as well as my family) have worked very hard your entire adult life and have "earned" and were promised very good health insurance. You and your family have the very best insurance plan there is. You have very low co-pays, you can go to whatever place that is approved for your "health" care. Your pharmaceutical prescriptions will be at a reduced price. You have most likely even paid into a government program that will aid in paying for your "health" care when you are retired and need medical services. However, you know this was coming..... their idea of "health" care and my idea of "health" care seem to be drastically different.

If you have never before heard this statement, let me be the first to share:

The worst thing you can have is the best insurance available.

Having said that, excellent insurance will help you pay; if you are waiting in the Emergency Room with your detached finger in a cooler. Yes, they will sew it back on and the finger will most likely even work again. Here in America, we have some amazing, top of the line, best Trauma Medical teams in the world. If you are in a horrible accident, they are the people to help. They can stitch up, remove bullets, repair broken limbs and so forth. That is where Trauma teams and insurance are extremely helpful and they shine.

There are certain times in our lives that we may need to rely on insurance and trauma teams to put Humpty Dumpty back together again.

If on the other hand, you are looking to heal yourself or your family naturally, that is going to be on your dime. You will have to take your purse out and pay for Thermography in place of a Mammogram. You will have to take out your wallet and pay for your own Magnesium Flakes. If you want to care for yourself during flu season, you will have to fork out the dollars for Elderberry powder in place of the "free" flu shot (your insurance company or our tax dollars pays the grocery store to offer). If you are interested in having the Mercury fillings removed from your teeth, you will have to save an envelope full of cash to do that.

On a positive productive note, insurance talk means to us....... the world is our oyster. The POSSIBILITIES are limitless as to how we can heal. I have read there are over 450 ways to heal from cancer. You just have to figure out what combination will work for you.

Dr. Simone Gold has developed an insurance program entitled Goldcare Health & Wellness that lends itself to helping those who choose to heal in a more natural way. www.goldcare.com

Marcus Ellis is a cancer thriver who has an organization (Viatical Settlements) that has a program to purchase life insurance policies and give you the money to use for natural healing from cancer. www.marcusellis.org

If your curiosity is peaked and you decided to read this book, you have incentive to find practical ways to implement natural healing into your lifestyle. Because medical insurance does not cover buying a masticating juicer that you will use every single day for 10 years or more.... the opportunities to THRIVE and take full ownership are right before you.

Just think how empowered you will feel? You took full ownership, you did the research, and you did the studying, you bought the organic apple...... you can do this.

Together, we can share ideas and ways to practically heal and thrive toward health and wellness. This is me CHEERING you on and applauding loudly!

Gentle Suggestion

Do not let traditional insurance steal the opportunity to thrive and take full ownership of your health.

Sunday's Child

Years ago, I came up with a gem of an idea. It helps me heal and it is fun, too.

One day a week, I declare, I am not sick.

You have most likely heard of folks who diet all week and then take one day a week to stop eating Cabbage Soup and half a grapefruit, and splurge on a Corn Dog, Pop Tarts, and Funyuns. In 1976 there was even a song by Larry Groce about a closet Junk food junkie. Okay, you understand where I am going with this. They are on a diet, yet one day a week they party like they have discovered the last box of Twinkies in a storm shelter. They basically thumb their noses at proper, healthy nutrition. (Remember, I offer NO judgment.)

I decided that Sunday would be my healthy day.

To begin with, I take one day a week off from taking any kind of supplements, vitamins, minerals and mushrooms. There are several studies citing the benefits of taking a break, one day a week, to allow your body to rest, recover and get ready for the week ahead.

One day a week, I do not study about health, healing, protocols and nutrition. I don't write about being sick. I don't talk about being sick. I do not answer any emails regarding my health. I don't take any phone calls from folks who want to ask me questions (I do schedule their calls for Monday.) I don't discuss my health journey with Mr. Right or anyone on that day. Even if I am sicker than a poor old dog on Saturday, come Sunday, I am fine and dandy.

On Sundays I might go to a museum. Occasionally I plan a picnic in the woods. We take a Sunday drive, remember those? We go to the mountain or the beach. Sometimes I ride my bike. Just like every other normal healthy person in the land. I might sit in a lawn chair and watch snazzy old cars cruise through our town. I look into finding a light house to visit. I may choose to kayak under a bridge or walk over a newly built structure. You never know, you might find me watching folks kite boarding on the Columbia River.

Did you ever think we might need to *practice* being healthy?

An international study found that smiling – even if it is posed or fake – can help improve mood and make people happier. It can also, reduce stress, increase levels of dopamine and serotonin. These are all adding up to what a healthy person might experience.

Wait! What if?

I am just posing a question here... What if, you *pretend* to be well? Will your body, mind and spirit know that it is just play acting OR will it actually believe you are healthy and vibrant?

Ragen Chastain says, "My answer is yes, "acting as if" can be a fantastic strategy for working on your intrinsic self-esteem". There you have it! We all know that a positive, self-esteem can do wonders for feeling and acting better.

> ## "I have chosen to be HAPPY because it is good for my health."
>
> VOLTAIRE

When you pretend you are not sick, you are smiling and taking beautiful nature photos. You write a happy, uplifting note to a friend. You try on and wear a sassy colored new lipstick. You have pep in your step. Healthy people go swimming. People who are full of life, get out the hula hoop and go a few rounds! Healthy people walk their dogs and say hello to neighbors. Folks that are vital have great posture. Healthy, thriving folks go barefoot while beachcombing. They talk about things they are working towards for the future. People with a strong constitution go river rafting. They try walking on stilts. People in the pink, pick flowers and make a crown. Some work on a jig saw puzzle. Healthful folks take a hike through a lava field, they dream a little. People who are flourishing make plans.

So, if you ever need a "let's go grab a coffee chum" or a partner in crime to check out the latest plants at a nursery, or visit a quilt shop to purchase some shockingly bright and cheerful fabric...you can count on me!

I am so focused finding Sunday goodness and happy, that my brain has no time to wonder to the darker side and fret.

> ## "It's the good girls who keep diaries; the bad girls never have the time."
>
> TALLULAH BANKHEAD

Sunday is the day that I spend determined to be grateful for what I have. I am gracious and use good manners all day long. I breathe. I hold hands with my guy.

I do not fret or grumble.

If I do feel an ache or pain, I will chalk it up to getting old, just like everyone else.

Gentle Suggestion

Please consider choosing one day a week to be vibrant,
hale and bubbling over with healthy exuberance.

Books

"Two roads diverged in a wood, and I took the one
less traveled by, and it has made all the difference."

ROBERT FROST

When we first stepped into this arena, we did what any human being would do, we of course went to the library.

I can distinctly remember the shoes I was wearing. Why? Once I found the cancer book section and I walked over, I saw the shelves and was assaulted by a sea of pink. Pink covers, pink ribbons, pink swishes......welcome to the sea of pink. I started crying. I was crying right in the public library. I can even remember the area of the library and what shelf it was on. I turned my head down and cried. I was looking at my sparkly, cute shoes. How could someone with really cute sparkle sneakers (to celebrate becoming a grandma for the first time) walk through this?

This is your life now; apparently you must embrace the pink.

I looked at each title. Not one, not one single book talked about hope, a road map to healing, or practical actions to take. They all talked about where to buy pink lipstick, where to purchase a wig, yes, you can eat anything you want, how to make it through chemotherapy and radiation. What are cancer treatments and how you will look like afterwards?

I felt and looked defeated. With my puffy eyes and splotchy red nose I went home, empty handed. Nothing quite as depressing as leaving a library empty handed. For once, my book bag with a colorful haughty elephant printed on the outside was empty on the inside.

On my next trip to the library, I went to a different section. I used different words: thriving, cancer, healing, wellness, hope, self-help etc. I found a few books and read all of those and tried to find more. Unfortunately, I wasn't keeping track then.

One morning, I poured a cup of coffee and sat down to the computer. Yes, that computer. The one that almost EVERY SINGLE PERSON said, "Don't look on the internet. You will just find quacks. You will find misinformation, hocus-pocus, lies, false hope; you would be a fool to put your health in the hands of the internet".

There are several different search engines that will help you learn about many natural healing choices and directions. Keep an open mind, do your own research, you might be surprised at what you will find outside the generally accepted biased portals. The raw data is out there, keep digging, you will find it.

Alternate Social Media platforms you might consider exploring:

www.brighteon.com, www.rumble.com, www.gab.com, www.telegram.com, www.truthsocial.com, www.clouthub.com, www.bitchute.com

I am typing a decade later and will transparently tell you that the internet and some of the information I gleaned, helped me SAVE MY LIFE.

I spend at least one hour a day, five days a week, eleven months a year, reading, researching, studying and taking notes. Each night over supper with Mr. Right, I review what I learned. We talk it over and swirl the ideas between us. I have been handed some brilliant information. I have found some great leads and yes, even some malarkey. I have watched TED talks, I have listened to podcasts, I have read book reviews, published papers and so forth.

Speaking of podcasts or talk shows, I highly recommend them. For example Robert Scott Bell www.robertscottbell.com among the many hats he wears, is a homeopathic practitioner, and shares a radio show, 2 hours a day, 6 days a week. You can turn it on and still quilt or stitch or prepare dinner. I have learned so much from him, his producer, Super Don and his guests. The information is there for the taking. Some episodes I am taking notes like a fourth grade girl learning new information. Other days I end up laughing or learning some history. Take some time to research and look into podcasts on health. Listening to an entertaining show is certainly an easy and convenient way to learn something new about our health.

While first seeking out health offering sources, I had to follow the trail to the money source. Now let me say, I am not opposed to selling a book. The author has shared information, research, tips that worked for them as well as studies that I want to learn from. I am willing to pay the price of a book to gain that knowledge. However, I am not interested in wasting my time, reading a "report" that was paid for by a company that will be selling a pharmaceutical drug and making a profit off of an unsubstantiated study. The "report" was paid for by them, for them.

Years ago, there was a popular book on the market called, "The Millionaire Next Door" written by Thomas Stanley. The thinking was/is if you want to be a millionaire do, think, eat, breathe, work, and save to be like one.

Couldn't I use that same strategy with cancer or any disease? If I want to gain my health back, thrive, play with my grandchildren, travel, and live a grateful life of wellness.....then I better find some books and people that show me how I can do just that.

I had to learn which sources and who I could trust. I also read some books with an opposite view point from mine as well. I needed to learn, hear and understand both sides.

The books that we have currently in our home library have been read, highlighted, dog eared, have green juice splotches, dropped in the bathtub, pen marks in the margins, creased, have been jammed into carry-on luggage, taken on trips, used with greasy hands, dirty hands, sand covered hands....in other words, our books have been used. We go back and re-read some. We re-read passages or paragraphs if we want to learn more, encourage ourselves or just drive home the point once more.

Some of the books were written by angels among us. Truly, angels who have walked over hot coals made it to the other side and are willing to share their knowledge with us. I have taken the time to write a thank you letter to some. Why? Because they have been instrumental in helping to hold my hand and save my life and I am mighty grateful.

To name a few angels who have walked among us:

Mike Adams, Dr. Bryan Ardis, Robert Scott Bell, Ty and Charlene Bollinger, Dr. Rashad Butar, Kris Carr, Charlotte Gerson, Bill Henderson, Dr. George

Malkmus, Dr. Judy Mikovits, Dr. Lee Merritt, Dr. Patrick Quillin, Dr. Mark Sircus, Chris Wark

We supported these courageous people. It took moxie to share their story and path chosen. All too often, courageous folks who chose the path less travelled are ridiculed and mocked. We buy their books. We support their efforts.

Now, that is not to say that I have liked each and every health and wellness book I have read. My goal is to learn at least one thing out of each book. On a couple of rare occasions, I have learned that some authors are not my cup of tea.

Sometimes, I can't put the book down. You get a feeling. This is the real deal. This information is going to make our lives better.

These are the books that have worked for us. We had to put the work in. We had to study, research, learn, take notes, memorized, implement and on the list goes.

Before I share my list, may I offer two suggestions?

With diligence, do your best to *keep an open mind*. We can learn something from everyone. Be it young or old, degree or not, even if you disagree 99.9% with what the person writes or believes, you and I can each learn something.

The one piece of information you uncover may "speak" to you and invoke a positive change in your health journey. Even if it goes against what you have already decided, changing your mind could help move you closer to good health.

> **"Be curious. It requires an active choice. When you encounter something you didn't know or that doesn't match your world view."**
>
> ROSE EVENLETH

The second suggestion is, *Be Curious*. Take a deep breath and calm down to help right the feeling of defensiveness or annoyance if you read something that doesn't quite match how you see the world.

I take full responsibility for my health.

> "Reading is essential for those who seek
> to rise above the ordinary."
>
> JIM ROHN

I am always open to hearing and learning about another author or book that I might gain some helpful knowledge from. I would love to hear from you and enter into an intelligent discussion about a book that has helped you.

The following are the names of books and authors who have inspired and helped to educated me along my path of health and healing:

Food Forensics by Mike Adams

Super Human by Dave Asprey

Life, Cancer, and God by Paula & Capt. Dale Black

The Cancer Survivors Guide by Neal D. Barnard, MD & Jennifer Reilly, MD

Unlock the Power to Heal by Robert Scott Bell & Ty Bollinger

Nutrition and You, About Selenium, One Cancer Answer by Chris Barr

Eat, Evolve, Advocate Transform by Kathy Mydlach Bero

Excitotoxins by Russell L. Blaylock, MD

Natural Strategies for Cancer Patients by Russell L. Blaylock, MD

31 Day Home Cancer Cure by Ty Bollinger

The Truth About Cancer by Ty Bollinger

Happy Healthy Thyroid by Andrea Beaman, HHC, AADP

Iodine, Why You Need It by David Brownstein, MD

Salt Your Way to Health by David Brownstein, MD

Active Against Cancer by Nancy S. Brennan

Crazy Sexy Cancer Tips by Kris Carr

Toxic Free by Debra Lynn Dadd

The Cancer Answer by Albert Carter & Larry Lymphocyte

Curing Cancer with Carrots by Ann Cameron

Reflexology by Inge Dougans

My Beef with Meat by Rip Esselstyn

Science and Health by Mary Baker Eddy

The Complete Guide to Fasting by Jason Fung, MD

The Gearson Therapy by Charlotte Gerson & Worton Walker, DPM

Sweet Poison by David Gilespie

How Not to Die by Michael Greger, MD

You can Heal your Life by Louise Hay

Cancer Free by Bill Henderson and Carlos M. Garcia, MD

The Copper Revolution by Jason Hommel

Stop Feeding Your Cancer by John Kelly, MD

The Earth Prescription by Laura Koniver, MD

First do no Harm by Rick Marschal, ND

God's Way to Ultimate Health by George H. Malkmis, MD

Ending Plague by Judy Mikovits, MD

Livin Good Daily by Blake Livingood, MD

Sea Salt's Hidden Powers by Jacques de Langre, Ph.D.

Shungite by Regina Martino

Upgrade your Immunity by Joseph Mercola, MD

EMF*D by Joseph Mercola, MD

Effortless Healing by Joseph Mercola, MD

How to Use Your Healing Power by Joseph Murphy, Ph.D., DD

The Liver & Gallbladder Miracle Cleanse by Andreas Moritz

Cancer Research Secrets by Keith Scott Mumbly, MD, Ph.D.

Why People Don't Heal and How They Can by Carline Myss, Ph.D.

The Tapping Solution by Nick Ortner

The Vitamin E Factor by Andreas Papas, Ph.D.

Outsmart Your Cancer by Tanya Harter Pierce

Do No Harm by Charles Pixley

Beating Cancer With Nutrition by Patrick Quillian, Ph.D., RD, CNS

The Wisdom and Healing Power of Whole Foods
by Patrick Quillian, Ph.D., RD, CNS

The New Good Life by John Robbins

Cure Your Fatigue (Copper) by Morley Robbins, MBA, CHC

The Empty Medicine Cabinet by Dustin Rudolph

In Bad Taste, the MSG Syndrome Complex by George
R. Schwartz & Kathleen A. Schwartz

The Cancer Industry by Mark Sloan

Cancer, The Metabolic Disease Unraveled by Mark Sloan

Red Light Therapy by Mark Sloan

The Ultimate Guide to Methylene Blue by Mark Sloan

Bath Bombs and Balneotherapy by Mark Sloan

Beyond the Arthritis Fix by Jason Hommel

The True Power of Hydrogen Peroxide by Mary Wright

The Revival Path to the New Earth, New Human by Penny Kelly

Healing with Iodine by Mark Sircus, MD

Cultured Foods for Health by Donna Schwenk

10 Essential Herbs by Lalitha Thomas

DIY Chlorine Dioxide by Brian Stone, Ph.D.

Budwig Protocol by Johanna Budwig

Transdermal Magnesium Therapy by Mark Sircus, MD

Radical Remission by Kelly A. Turner, Ph.D.

The Sound of Healing by Michael Tyrrell

Choosing a Natural Immunomodulator by Vaclav Vetvicka, Ph.D.

The ph Miracle by Robert O. Young, Ph.D.

Chris Beat Cancer by Chris Wark

Square One by Chris Wark

Beat Cancer Daily by Chris Wark

Anxiety-Free with Food by Liana Werner-Gray

Cancer-Free with Food by Liana Werner-Gray

Killing Cancer Not People by Robert G. Wright

Herbal Medicine by Katja Swift

Herbal Recipes for Vibrant Health by Rosemary Gladstar

Medicinal Herbs by Rosemary Gladstar

Earthing by Clinton Ober, Stephen T. Sinatra, MD & Martin Zucker

Plague of Corruption by Judy Mikovits, MD

The Invisible Fatal Conveniences that are Making us Sick by Darin Olien

Gentle Suggestion

Always be reading.

Yuck

Sometime in the 1970's my mother used stickers called Mr. Yuck. It was a circle outlined in black with a neon green background. The image was a sick looking face with a tongue sticking out. If a product had harmful chemicals and we were not supposed to touch, she put a sticker on the item, front and center. YUCK don't touch!

Think of this list as the Mr. Yuck of cosmetics and some household products. Please due your due diligence to read, learn and then make the effort to remove the yucky chemicals from your home and lifestyle.

A fantastic resource is the Environmental Working Group. www.ewg.org They have thousands of products listed in databases. To find safer soaps, shampoos and make up products, you simply type in the product name and they rate it for its level of chemicals or health. To discover what is good and what is yuck, I have found this free web site to be an extremely helpful tool.

Also, The David Suzuki foundation www.davidsuzuki.org is another excellent source for further, in-depth, information on harmful products.

The following is an abbreviated list of some unhealthy chemicals that may have contributed to my ill health, and quite possibly yours.

By becoming informed and scrupulous label readers, and avoiding the dirty dozen food chemicals and many more, may we all become more vibrant, cleaner and healthier humans.

- **SLS (Sodium Laurel Sulfate)**

Makes products bubble and foam, has measurable amounts of ethylene oxide and dioxane, human carcinogens

- **BHA and BHT (Butylated hydroxyanisole, Butylated hydroxytoluene)**

Preservatives in lipsticks and moisturizers, food preservatives

Interferes with hormone function, tumor promoter and possible human carcinogens

- **DEA (Diethanolamine)**

Used to make cosmetics creamy or sudsy, contributes to liver cancer, and precancerous changes in skin and thyroid, human carcinogens

- **Formaldehyde**

Releasing agents used in a wide range of cosmetics, plastics, vinyl flooring, permanent press fabrics, mattresses, furniture...

Human carcinogen

- **Coal Tar Dyes**

Used extensively in cosmetics and hair dye

Human carcinogens

- **Parabens**

Preservatives in cosmetics, fragrance ingredients interferes with hormone function, possible association between cosmetics and cancer

- **Perfume (fragrance)**

Cosmetic ingredients, perfumes (over 3,000 chemicals), colognes, deodorants, laundry detergents, cleaning products

Did you know, even products marketed as "fragrance-free" or "unscented" may in fact contain fragrance along with a masking agent that prevents the brain from perceiving odor? Wow, this was a surprise to me.

Interferes with hormone function, toxic to wild life

- **PEG compounds (polyethylene glycols)**

Used in cosmetics as thickeners, solvents, softeners, moister carriers

Human carcinogen, harms nervous system

- **Petrolatum**

Cosmetic moisturizers and hair care products

Human carcinogen

- **Polysorbate 80**

Solubilize ingredients, irate eyes, skin, allergies, developmental toxicity, reproductive toxicity, liver toxicity, carcinogenic

- **Siloxanes (Silicone based compounds)**

Moisturizers, facial treatments, soften, smooth, make deodorants slide, medical implants

Uterine tumors, harm to reproductive and immune system

- **Triclosan**

Used in antiperspirants/deodorants, cleaners, hand sanitizers, laundry detergent, and facial tissues

Interferes with hormone function

Gentle Suggestion

Buy yourself a fancy hand held magnifying glass. Or on your next trip to the $1.25 store buy a pair of readers. To fit the long list of chemicals on a label, the print has become scaled down. The companies that are making a profit are hoping you don't buy the illuminated magnifying glass.

Wellness Products and Websites Directory

The following is a list of Wellness products and websites that I have used and been pleased with services rendered.

As of this, August 2023 writing all listings are current and conducting business.

Berkey Water filter	www.usaberkeyfilters.com
Beta Glucan	www.ancient5.com
Black Raspberries	www.berrihealth.com
Blue Bottle Love	www.bluebottlelove.com
Ty and Charlene Bollinger	www.thetruthaboutcancer.com
Chaga	www.birchboys.com
Chris Wark	www.chrisbeatcancer.com
David Suzuki Foundation	www.davidsuzuki.org
Dead Sea Minerals	www.deadseawarehouse.com
Earthing	www.earthing.com
Environmental Working Group	www.ewg.org
Essiac Tea	www.essiacproducts.com
Fermented foods	www.culturedfoods.com
Frank Cousineau	www.cancercontrolsociety.org
Grains and Grit	www.grainsandgrit.com
Grounding	www.groundingofficial.com
Harmony 783	www.harmony783.com

Kris Carr	www.Kriscarr.com
Lee Merritt, M.D	www.themedicalrebel.com
Level Up Way (hydrogen water)	www.levelupway.com
Level up Way	www.levelupwy.com
Methylene Blue	www.endalldisease.com
Mountain Rose Herb	www.mountainroseherb.com
Mushrooms	www.hostdefensecom
Natural Sweetener products	www.waxorchards.com
Orange Guard	www.orangeguard.com
Organic popcorn	www.amishcountrypopcorn.com
Red Light Therapy	www.mitoredlight.com
Richway Biomat	www.biomats.com
Silverite pillow	www.silveriteglobal.com
Vermont Salt Cave Spa	www.vtsaltcaves.com
Zenith Supplies	www.zenithsupplies.com

Protocols

YOU must do your own research, beyond the information I share. I mean, get down and dirty, take notes, read past the buzzing timer, find several sources, do your very best to learn and then learn some more.

When you do discuss a protocol with your allopathic doctor, odds are, he or she is busy person. They have chosen not to take the time to research and study many of the naturopathic ways to heal. Before you bring your questions up, you must be well versed and thoroughly convinced of their efficacy.

Remember your goal is to heal and thrive. Please don't expend your limited healing energy trying to convince someone of a certain protocol. The only people you *can* "convince" are those who have already walked down the path less traveled and are thriving today.

You may need to take a moment or a couple days and breathe before you share what you are thinking about trying. Whether it is a friend, an allopathic medically trained person, relative, neighbor or close family member....be forewarned, they may not be as excited and receptive to this "unheard of" "crazy" "undocumented" idea as you had hoped.

Many folks seem to think because you have decided not to partake in chemotherapy and radiation that you are just thumbing your nose at that protocol with your coat tails flapping, you are just flouncing away, choosing to do nothing.

Quite frankly, nothing could be farther from the truth. I am here to tell you, it would be much easier, quicker, with no thinking or learning involved if you just sign on the dotted line and followed their orders.

Don't ask questions, do not ask for efficacy results, don't ask about side-effects (now or residual), do no studying, no reading, no learning, now or down the line, just follow along and do as they say. Case closed.

When your case is closed and you have followed along and participated in 6 months, 9 months or 52 weeks of their protocol, you will be rewarded with you ringing a bell, a cheering clapping medical staff, a certificate of completion and of course the all elusive and hoped for words... "*You are cured*".

I will be honest and say, the nice neat package of an ending date and never think about it again, go back to your regularly scheduled life and eat and live like you were......is very enticing.

However, once the genie is out of the bottle it is difficult to put her back inside.

The less travelled, less talked about, gentle natural path is a bit quieter. No bell ringing, no cheering staff. There is no going out for a cheeseburger, diet coke and mud pie to celebrate.

"All of my knowledge is learned by standing on the shoulders of geniuses."

ALBERT SCHWEIZTZER

Each of the protocols I list has a vast library of information which is available. Each has been proven over many years to work on all types of cancer (as well as other ailments and diseases).

I highly recommend the book Cancer Free (Your guide to Gentle, Non-toxic Healing) by Bill Henderson and Carlos M. Garcia, MD. They have written extensively with very descriptive explanations of several protocols.

Also, highly recommended the book, Chris Beat Cancer by Chris Wark.

He, too, lists and reviews many protocols and methods that are in the natural genre. He also has a vibrant social media presence, many You-Tube videos, and interviews with people who are thriving, as well as a program called Step One.

Because of so many family members receiving a diagnosis, Ty and Charlene Bollinger have walked over the coals and felt called to share solutions and remedies with the world. I am here to tell you, they took that to heart. A font of information can be discovered at The Truth About Cancer.

www.thetruthaboutcancer.com Ty has a book by the same name and they have gone on to produce documentaries that will elevate your life and fill your cup to overflowing with solid researched information, encouragement, and faith.

These angels among us have shared well researched, solid helpful information about many, many healing choices that are available. I will not try to re-write and match their beautiful research. It is available for the taking.

I will list some of the protocols that I have used. Several of these modalities I have used for 6 years or more. In the same breath, I will say, that others, I have tried for a sincere 6 month period and decided it was time to move on to something different.

This is where nobody tells you what to do. YOU have the privilege to learn and decide what combination will work for you. The power to choose is one of the greatest gifts we have as human beings.

> "The great thing about life-the most magnificent thing about being these sentient human beings-is that we have been given the power of choice."
>
> BRYANT MCGILL

The Budwig Protocol, Dr. Joanna Budwig was nominated for seven Nobel prizes during her 50 plus years of advocacy. She was a brilliant star with much to offer the world.

For more information please see: www.BudwigCenter.com

Kick-Ass Red Cowgirl boots, oh yes, you read that correctly. I always wanted a pair. I am not a farmer, nor a horse rider, nor am I a country western concert attendee. Although, once years ago, myself and some other church wives "tricked" our husbands (her husband already said yes sort of thing) into taking country western dance lessons. Haha... Anyway, the protocol I am talking about is timing. Do not put it off. This is your sign for you to buy that cashmere sweater you have pined over. If you have always dreamed of buying those red soled high heeled shoes...... now is the time. Save up, make it a priority. Even if you only wear them once or twice, I guarantee you that every single time you see those beauties winking at you from inside your closet, you WILL smile! This is your moment. That purchase will create a sense of health and happiness that nothing else will.

The Hallelujah Diet (vegan and raw food), Barley Powder, Rev. Dr. George Malkmus shares a Christian foundation for eating the way God intended.

For more information please see:
www.myhdiet.com and www.GreenSupreme.net

Gerson Therapy Charlotte Gerson was an amazing human. There are several clinics that implement her vision for healing.

For more information please see: www.heal.hope4cancer.com

Essiac Tea, shared by Rene Caisse The formula had been passed up through the Ojibwa Indian Tribe's medicine men. In 1922 it landed in the hands of a Canadian nurse named Rene.

For more information please see: www.essiac-canada-intl.com

Chlorine Dioxide, an in-depth study by Brian Stone, PhD, MBA

Methylene Blue, Dr. Joseph Mercola, Mark Sloan

For More information please see: www.endalldisease.com

Protocel

For more information please see:
www.ElonnaMcKibben.com and www.OutsmartYourcancer.com

Far Infrared Therapy

For more information please see: Richway Biomat www.biomats.com

Red Light Therapy www.mitoredlight.com

Amygdalin, Laetrile, Vitamin B17, Apricot Seeds

For more information please see: author G. Edward Griffin, World Without Cancer

John Richardson (whose father was an inspiration for G. Edward Griffin to write the book) now runs the foundation www.RNC.com Out of 1200 foods that you can eat, Apricot seeds have the highest level of Amygdalin.

Fenbendazole

For more information please see: www.fenbendazole.org

Sodium bicarbonate, Magnesium , Dr. Mark Sircus

As Bill Henderson said, "Do not trust the "system" to take care of you or your loved one's cancer. Get Proactive. DO THE RESEARCH. Get Knowledge. Knowledge is power."

My list is ever changing and continues on...I am striving for vital health and wellness.

Gentle Suggestion

"Knowledge is not power, it is only potential.
Applying that knowledge is power."

TAKEDA SHINGEN

Words not Worms

The words we use and hear evoke emotions and have tremendous energy and power.

Words have the power to hinder, hurt, harm and humiliate. If you believe that, then you must believe the flip side of that coin. Words also have the ability to offer hope and healing.

"Words are powerful. Whether you write or speak them, they do have an impact on you and others. Words can change someone's mood completely and ignite a spark in them." www.voicesofyouth.org

Words can save a life; they can free a soul, they can bring happiness to one's day, never underestimate the healing power of words.

"Your body hears everything your mind says."

NAOMI JUDD

If you believe that words can indeed heal, then let's begin right now. You are going to want to write on the bathroom mirror or window to your backyard, so grab a colorful Chalk Marker.

If you are keeping a Healing Journal, you can use your retractable colorful Gel pens to write your favorite quotes.

When you write words down on paper, you start to enable a higher level of thinking.

Each day I choose a different quote, verse, affirmation or spirit lifter to ponder, memorize, and repeat. Words to lift my spirits, give me Practical Hope, something that gently reminds me that I am going in the right direction. Sometimes even a short quote to help me make it through a meltdown.

I have even seen the results of someone writing down the quote, embellished with markers and doodles and then added it to their refrigerator doors on a daily basis. The doors are covered and boy howdy is it inspirational.

You are welcome to borrow a couple or all of mine. You will undoubtedly add to the list. Hopefully you will be encouraged to write new and inspiring quotes in the margins.

The following are some of the positive quotes; motivational thoughts and affirmations that have helped guide me along the way. Please keep going and add some of your own.

Ps. For a giggle, change all the times I typed "words" on this page and replace with "worms". Okay, that's funny. (Remember, laughter heals.)

Does your spirit need a lift? I've got you covered.

Each of us possesses the divine gift of self healing.

"You have the power to heal your life and you need to know that."

LOUISE L. HAY

"A cheerful heart is good medicine"

PROVERBS 12:22

"I am in the right place, at the right time, doing the right thing."

LOUISE L. HAY

"The natural healing force in each one of us is the greatest force in getting well."

HIPPOCRATES

"When fear disappears, the foundation of disease is gone."

MARY BAKER EDDY

I am Worthy of Good Health.

"For I will restore health to you, and your
wounds I will heal, declares the Lord."

JEREMIAH 30:17

"Lord my God, I called to you for help, and you healed me."

PSALM 30:2

I am a Magnificent Soul with Unlimited Healing Potential.

"The Power to Heal is yours."

ROBERT SCOTT BELL

"I am worthy of the time it takes to do the things that heal."

MORGAN HARPER NICHOLS

Your body's ability to heal is greater than
anyone has permitted you to believe.

Each of us possesses the Divine gift of self healing.

"I am willing to release the pattern within me
that is creating this experience or condition."

LOUISE HAY

"As long as you can hear the words, there is Hope."

TUCKER CARLSON

"The very least you can do in your life is figure out what you hope for. And the most you can do is live inside that hope. Not admire it from a distance but live in it, under its roof."

BARBARA KINGSOLVER

"Let your hopes, not your hurts, shape your future."

ROBERT H. SCHULLER

"...He healed them."

MATTHEW 15:30

Gentle Suggestion

Lean into positive thoughts.

Allow yourself to be SPLASHED with Grace, Goodness and Healing.

Circle the Wagons

At the end of a long journey, the camp circle is calling – good news and relief, everyone is welcome.

In the camp circle there are people with messy hair hidden under bandanas. The circle consists of good hearty & hale folks, who you would gladly eat chow or trail mix with. The people around the circle are relaxed souls who are wearing dusty sneakers or Kick-Ass red cowgirl boots, each person with dirty fingernails from rearranging & balancing rocks. Several have dirty faces; from the heat of the fire and the journey, each has rosy cheeks. Everyone has a stick. Each unique stick is to roast something, to stare aimlessly into the flames and watch the end glow red or to write in the dirt, their name and hopes.

There are very few people in your life that help you remember there is hope. Just by the sound of their voice you can hear the courage they are sharing or the smile they are offering.

> **"Good friends help you to find important things when you have lost them... your smile, your hope and your courage."**
>
> DOE ZANTAMATA

I don't have to explain to anyone that life gets messy. Folks that are willing to saddle up, those brave enough to jump on the teeter-totter, raise chickens, or when your gut tells you to walk silently away, these are the very people that sometimes have dirty hands and hearts that hurt from honest to goodness work and troubles.

If you choose to hide out, stay quiet, follow traditional rules, not jump into the deep end, then maybe for you, life isn't so messy?

The second group is not my tribe. *I can tell my tribe by their tear streaked, messy faces.*

Maybe that's it? Maybe I don't have to explain anything messy to my Camp Circle friends? They know messy. Now and then, I just need to hear their voices and borrow a little bit of their hard earned courage. While holding my coffee mug with two hands, I lean in to hear a smidgen of hope in their voice.

I don't want to live on the edge of other people's happiness. I want to sit around the fire in mismatched lawn chairs. I want to grab a bit of their happy and mix it in the dirt with my happy.

My goal is to find or make a reason to celebrate being healthy, vibrant and grateful every single day.

Sharing those goals with ridiculously smart, brave, creative, vibrant camp friends would be a bonus.

I have been scared, mad, shed tears, brought to my knees and found myself in way over my head. Little by little I have found ways to tip the balance to create a healthy, vibrant courageous life. I have spent hours finding answers.

My goal in writing this book was twofold. First, I needed to release the hate, ugliness, anger, loneliness, frustration, hurt, sadness, guilt, and trouble from my heart.

"Let not your heart be troubled."

JOHN 14: 1-3

The second reason was, to come up with a way to share some of my courage and above all Practical Hope with you.

"The final stage of healing is using what happens to you to help other people."

GLORIA STEINEM

Sincere and heartfelt thanks for reading this book and allowing me to use what happened to me to offer you Practical Hope.

I solemnly promise nothing you can tell me will make me cower and run. I know what courage is. I know what it feels like. While wearing polished Loafers, I have felt the heat as I walked over the hot coals, and I am here to tell you there is HOPE.

I am mighty grateful for YOU my disheveled, curious, bandana wearing, tear streaked, fellow campers. No one I would rather be messy with.

I will not waver.

I am standing right here offering you Practical Hope.

In this together, friends.

Here's to our good health!

Gentle Suggestion

Saddle up, daylight's burning.

Dear God,

May this book be of service.

Your humble servant,

Daleen

Acknowlegements

Sincere thanks to Mr. Tom Paciello for offering to do the first, messy edit. I appreciate and respect your candor, corrections, suggestions and humor. You sir, are a scholar and a gentleman. I am grateful to have you in my corner.

My heartfelt thanks to Mrs. Barbara Braun for your offer to do the first read through. Even though you are much too nice and kind to criticize harshly, your suggestions, thoughts and inquiries helped encourage me to keep heading for the finish line. I value and I am grateful for your friendship. I would sit around a camp fire with you anytime.

Thank you to Mrs. Laura Gravina for your insight, intelligence and humor. You found a way to encourage me to finish the book. I appreciate the research that you do. You helped me realize that there are indeed other folks in my tribe.

Sincere thanks to Mr. Joe Hurst. You met with me in Nashville in early 2020. You acted like my book was going to happen. You asked questions and offered suggestions. You were the first human outside Mr. Right, who talked like this was a reality. I appreciate and am thankful for your encouragement, honesty, humor and insight. You made me actually think I could write a book.

Thanks to my elementary school friend, Mrs. Teresa Wingard. I admire your listening skills. Thank you for not thinking I was crazy. I appreciate you asking questions and offering encouragement. I am grateful and fortunate to have you in my circle.

To my son, Gabe Wilson, your skills as a Graphic Designer never cease to amaze me. I appreciate your creative and whimsical brain. Your passion and talent created a book cover that I am proud of. (I guess all those "I'm bored" days that I suggested you go and paint, color or draw...paid off!) Heartfelt thanks for using your time, energy and spirit for this project. I am so proud of you.

To my husband, Bruce Wilson, first and foremost sincere thanks for trying to explain computer technology even though you know I am not even remotely interested. Thank you for the amazing amount of patience you implore with my swirly brain. Thank you for offering suggestions even though I did not agree with everything. Thank you for putting up with and working with me at 8:30 pm, when we both know full well you would rather help me at 5:30 am. Heartfelt thanks for helping to make this book a reality. I am the luckiest girl in the world to have found my Mr. Right.

Author Biography

Following a cancer diagnosis with 6 months to live, I said no thank you to chemotherapy and radiation. I chose a path less traveled, less accepted.

Ten plus years later and I am standing right here, offering practical hope.

Maker, soul tender, wife, mom, granny, Godmother, gardener, bread baker, bike rider, chicken keeper, cross stitcher, quilter, plant eater and grateful thriver.

I share insight, suggestions, ideas, lists and above all practical hope.

I live in the Pacific Northwest with Mr. Right, chickens and our three-year-old, English Cream Retriever, Amazing Grace "Mazie".

info@practical-hope.com